GREATER

Than

YOURSELF

GREATER

Than

YOURSELF

The Ultimate Lesson of
True Leadership

> > > > > > > > >

STEVE FARBER

DOUBLEDAY

NEW YORK LONDON TORONTO

SYDNEY AUCKLAND

DD

DOUBLEDAY

Published in the United States by Doubleday, an imprint of The Doubleday Publishing Group, a division of Random House, Inc., New York.
www.doubleday.com

Cataloging-in-Publication Data is on file with the Library of Congress.

ISBN 978-0-385-52261-8

PRINTED IN THE UNITED STATES OF AMERICA

20 19 18 17 16 15 14 13 12

PART I

by Patrick Lencioni

Author of *The Five Dysfunctions of a Team*

The most memorable sports event of my youth occurred when I was in fifth grade during the one-mile run at the regional Junior Olympics. I'll never forget the exhilaration I felt at winning against the odds, and the joy that our entire family experienced that day.

I went on to have lots of athletic successes—scoring runs, making baskets, winning races. I even went on to run track competitively in college. But there was something about those Junior Olympics that stands out in my mind. It has to do with the fact that it wasn't me running the race that day, but my big brother, Vince.

There is something about watching someone you admire and love succeed that surpasses the feelings of satisfaction that come from your own success. This is at the heart of the practice that Steve Farber calls Greater Than Yourself, and as I've grown older, I've come to understand it more and more.

That is not to say that I'm unappreciative of my own accomplishments. I am thankful to God and feel truly blessed that I have been able to experience some success as an author, speaker, and consultant, and to have an impact on people in ways that I could not have imagined earlier in my career. But it wasn't until I met a young man named Matthew that I realized the power of lifting someone else above me, someone, I believed, whose mission and potential exceeded my own.

Years ago I was working with an executive team in Minnesota, and after the two-day session one of the team members asked me if I had heard of a young Australian author named Matthew Kelly. When I admitted that I hadn't, he recommended that I check him out.

Now, I get many recommendations from clients and friends, but because of my hectic work and home schedule, and the fact that I spend a lot of time writing books of my own, I don't often follow up. But for some reason, this recommendation seemed different.

So I ordered one of Matthew Kelly's books, read it a few weeks after it arrived, and had my world turned upside down. For the next nine months I thought about calling Matthew personally to tell him how much his book meant to me, and to see what kind of guy he was. It took nine months for me to make that call because I secretly feared that he might not be the person I imagined him to be—how could he be? Nonetheless, I finally made the call and learned that Matthew was familiar with my books, and had read one of them and used it with his team. He had even called his agent at the time and said that he wanted to write a book with me someday! That blew me away.

Next, I decided to hear Matthew speak, so I arranged to travel to another city to attend one of his talks. Until that point in my life I had never done anything like that—not for a concert or a football game, and certainly not to hear someone give a lecture. I mean, that's what *I* do for a living. And with three kids at home and another on the way, how could I justify such a trip?

But I went, with my wife's blessing, and found myself overcome with enthusiasm for Matthew and his message. This made little sense to me at the time. After all, Matthew was younger than me by almost eight years. And he was speaking to a relatively small, unsophisticated audience, in a smaller, less sophisticated venue than I was used to working in. And yet, what he was saying and the way he was saying it made it clear to me that I had to help him in whatever way I could. So when his talk was over, I threw on one of those vendor's aprons and joined his staff selling his books to attendees at the event. And it was wonderful!

I remember telling my wife when I went home the next day that I think that one of God's purposes for me in my life was to help people get to know Matthew Kelly and his work. Then she read his books and understood why.

Well, then came my next big Matthew Kelly experience. I decided to bring Matthew Kelly to my town to speak. And so, for the next three or four months, I went around the area talking to people and handing out flyers and networking with anyone who would listen about Matthew and the power of his message. I worked harder at that event than I did at my own job, and worried about it more, too.

When Matthew came, he addressed a truly packed house, caused a traffic jam on the freeway leading to the venue, and changed more than a thousand people's lives with his talk. As that talk ended and he went to sign books (which is what I'm usually doing in situations like that), I felt a sense of purpose and accomplishment and joy that I had never experienced before in my own lectures and speeches.

Next, I introduced Matthew to the organizers of a conference where I speak. Based on my enthusiasm for him and his message, they reviewed his tape and decided to include him in their next conference. What an amazing experience for me, to be speaking at the same event with my friend Matthew.

Well, Matthew and I both gave our regular talks at the conference. And during the break as we walked out into the lobby, people streamed right past me to tell Matthew what a wonderful job he did. And you know how that made me feel? Strangely enough, exhilarated.

How could this be? How could I feel such a sense of accomplishment and satisfaction helping someone who was younger than I was, and in many ways lesser known, achieve more recognition and attention than I did? How could I want someone else to be greater than myself? As much as we like to believe that we are capable of such actions, I have to admit that I was surprised by it all.

But as I look back at my life, at the people I've rooted for harder than myself, I recognize what it is that makes this all possible. First, I have to love the person; I loved my brother. Part of loving other people has to do with admiring them, seeing qualities and skills and talents in them that, objectively speaking, surpass my own. My brother was a better runner than me. And then I have to believe that what they are doing is more important than what I am doing. My brother was representing our family in a world where we were novices.

He was the only runner on the track that day at the Junior Olympics without spikes; we were unknown to most of the people there.

Matthew Kelly is speaking and writing about topics that are eternally more important than my own. He has an ability to see and describe those topics in ways that I cannot. And through the last few years, I have come to love Matthew as a friend.

This book is going to challenge you to find your own Greater Than Yourself relationships—to invest in another person in a way that raises him or her above yourself. At first it may seem counterintuitive, maybe even unnatural, but I encourage you to set aside your preconceived notions of success and accomplishments and throw yourself wholeheartedly into the GTY endeavor, as I've done with Matthew. Soon you'll find yourself asking very different questions about the relationships in your life, at work and at home.

For me, I've come to realize that the question I ask myself shouldn't be "How can I want someone else to be greater than myself, and how can I be more enthusiastic about someone else's work and career than about my own?" The question should be "How can I not?"

PART II

by Matthew Kelly
Author of *The Dream Manager*

By the time Pat Lencioni came into my life, I had been speaking and writing successfully for more than a decade; sadly, I had become used to people wanting things from me. Pat's genuine lack of self-interest, combined with his overwhelming desire to help me pursue and fulfill my destiny in this life, were incredibly refreshing and disarming from the very beginning. It is the kind of relationship that restores your faith in humanity, and the future that might be possible for our children and grandchildren.

Just reading what Pat has written in this foreword is humbling. But actually experiencing the relationship he has described has been one of the great lessons of my life.

The question I would like to ponder with you is this. What makes someone capable of a Greater Than Yourself relationship? The answer we find alive and well in the life and person of Pat Lencioni.

To be capable of a Greater Than Yourself relationship, you need two things: (1) humility, and (2) a firm and evolving sense of who you are and what you are here for. Pat has both, although I doubt you'll ever hear him describe himself that way.

The truth, though, is that many people don't have the foggiest idea about their sense of self. Too many of us spend too much of our lives pretending to be someone we are not, or trying to be someone we think others want us to be. And humility, well, that is about the rarest thing on earth today, and yet it is the single thing that is most effective at tearing down the prejudices and biases that separate us. Humility is the key to all personal and interpersonal unity.

The paradox, and it seems there always is one, is that you can best acquire these abilities by dedicating yourself to a GTY relationship. The most effective way to learn and grow is to go out and actually do the very things we are trying to learn.

There is one more powerful insight that my relationship with Pat has taught me. My initial reaction to Pat's enthusiastic support, and his selfless contribution to my life and work, was to want to do something for him. I wanted to repay him. I wanted to give to him in the measure he had given to me. Over time I realized that I was acting from the wrong relationship paradigm. Today I am looking for the person that I am called to have a Greater Than Myself relationship with, someone I can devote myself to in the way Pat has done with me. That, I've come to realize, is the very best way I can "repay" him.

Most relationships in life and in business are based upon a mutual give and take. But a GTY relationship goes way beyond this social norm. And in doing so, it promises to raise every person, situation, and organization to a new level.

So read this book, and then live this book. I think both Steve and Pat would agree with me that too many books are written, too many books are read, and too few books are lived. Please don't make that mistake with *Greater Than Yourself*.

This book is my third contribution to the increasingly popular genre known as the "business parable." As in my previous two books, *The Radical Leap* and *The Radical Edge,* I've played fast and loose with the boundaries between imagination and reality. While the principles behind the practice of Greater Than Yourself are, in essence, ancient, timeless truths, the characters I've employed to communicate these truths are—how can I put this nicely—not.

Same goes for the story.

But there's a wrinkle. While the book is mostly a fictional set of events occurring between my imaginary friends and me, some of the story you are about to read is true.

Specifically, references to my own life's history, my guitar, and my relationship with the person you will soon meet as my "GTY Project" are as real as it gets (visit GreaterThanYourself.com to see what I mean). But if you send me an e-mail requesting the contact information for Charles Roland, Cat Cassidy, or Gene Zander, you'll be as dismayed as the day you found Santa's beard in the laundry bin next to Mommy's frilly thing.

You will also get a snarky reply from me asking you to go

back and read this introduction, which, obviously, you would not have done.

So, with that out of the way, I invite you to dive in and experience the transformational nature of the Greater Than Yourself principle in the very real, nonfiction story that really matters.

Yours.

GREATER

Than

YOURSELF

The obsession seized me with all the subtlety of a sumo wrestler hopped up on anabolics.

I'd been playing guitar for thirty-five years, and I'd owned a couple of decent ones from time to time, but suddenly I needed—*needed*—that 1959 Gibson hollow-body electric hanging on the rack at Vintage Brothers Guitars in Carlsbad, California.

I don't know what it was. I'd seen nicer guitars, to be sure. There was nothing unusual about its sunburst finish, and with only one pickup in the middle position, the ES-330 wasn't considered the most desirable of collectible instruments. But other than a few minor nicks on the headstock, it was in perfect condition, and as I sat in the store's small demo room, playing it hour after hour, I fell deeper and deeper in love. The neck was fast, the tone, sweet, rich, and mellow. Yeah, I was in love, man, but not all love and obsession wind up in marriage, so eventually I put it back on the rack, inquired just one more time about the price, and walked out into the salty San Diego, Pacific Ocean air.

I've played better guitars, I kept telling myself, and I've seen better deals on vintage instruments. But as I walked toward my car, I couldn't shake it. Then the sumo got me, spun me around, and shoved me back down the parking lot from where I'd come. My pace quickened as I approached the shop, and my wallet was out before I even got through the door. I paid the price—about the cost of a decent European vacation—grabbed the case, and, minutes later, grinning a grin that tested the limits of my cheek muscles, I tucked that baby into the passenger seat and buckled it in like the prize it was.

I had to have that guitar. *Had* to.

And now, just a few days later, I know why.

I'm not really sure what to call it when things line themselves up without my slightest knowledge or influence. It's as if someone is executing a preconceived plan to make all the random pieces of my life fit together. What is it? Karma? Kismet? Synchronicity? I don't know, but it happens to me a lot, and more often than not it works out well. I just seem to meet the right teachers at the right time.

I've been blessed (maybe that's the word) with the opportunity to work with some of the world's preeminent thinkers in business leadership—like Tom Peters and Jim Kouzes, to name a couple. And in recent years, under extremely odd and seemingly fortuitous circumstances, I've learned directly from some of the masters of what I've come to know as Extreme Leadership—like William Maritime and Agnes Golden and Ted Garrison, names that'll be familiar to readers of my previous books. All of them, in their own ways, taught me that real leadership is not about calling yourself "leader"; rather, it's about taking up the cause to change some piece of the world for the better. Real leadership, in other words, is an extreme act rooted in love and motivated by a desire to create a better world—whether it's the world of your company, team, neighborhood, or family. Simply put, real leadership *is* Extreme Leadership.

I've done a pretty good job of conveying the Extreme Leadership lessons I've learned along the way, and I think that's why I've made a bit of a name for myself in certain circles. Some have even used the words *Steve Farber* and *leadership guru* in the same sentence, which, although gratifying to my ego, makes me squirm like I have a load of wet worms in my socks.

Right teachers. Right time. Odd circumstances.

I was thinking I should print that on my business card, because it seemed to happen over and over again.

I was back in my apartment on the bay side of the Mission Beach area of San Diego. The ocean and its frenetic boardwalk were a couple of blocks to the west, but calm, tranquil Mission Bay lay just a few short yards to the east of my building, affording a view through my living room window worthy of a tourist's postcard.

I had returned from Carlsbad a couple of hours earlier, cleared my agenda by taking care of a few time-bound tasks, and was now—finally!—ready to spend some quality time getting intimate with my new companion.

I gingerly placed the tattered, half-a-century-old, mottled brown guitar case on the dining room table. I flipped open the latches, lifted the top, and let my gaze linger over the sunburst-colored curves of my new six-string babe.

Sitting on a bar stool with the guitar propped in my lap, I twisted the tuning knobs until the sound was just right, and fired off a couple of quick blues licks in the key of E. I'd plug it in later; for now I was enjoying the smooth feel of the Brazilian rosewood fingerboard and the muted, rich sound resonating off its unamplified, maple body. I was just about to settle in for a couple of hours of serious playing (which sounds like an oxymoron—but it's not) when something in the case caught my eye. I set the guitar in a stand and got up to take a closer look.

The pink, plush lining on the inside bottom of the case was pulled slightly back at the seam. A small, yellowed piece of paper stuck out from under the fabric. I pinched the corner and pulled on it gently. It slid easily from under the velvet and revealed itself to be a handwritten note.

I felt a voyeuristic jolt similar to what an archaeologist must feel when finding a relic offering a glimpse into another's life, in another time.

"Dear Jessica," the note began. "This guitar is my gift to you. It was made in 1959, thirty-one years before I taught you your first lesson. What a player you've become in just five short years. Now that you're old enough to vote and on your way to school and the distractions of adult life, you'll need this guitar to remind you of your wonderful musical gift. May it help you to become a better player than I could ever hope to be. I have no doubt you will.

"You have brought this old teacher of yours more joy than you could possibly know. I want you to know that I'm very, very proud of you.

"Your friend and teacher, GZ."

"You've been around, haven't you?" I said to the guitar in the stand.

I read the note one more time and tried to imagine the teacher, the student, and the strong bond that had obviously existed between them. It was an unusual thing, that kind of connection. I'd been lucky enough to experience that student-teacher bond in my professional life, and I knew how rare and priceless a thing it could be, so, naturally, I found myself wondering where these people were today and what, if anything, had happened with Jessica's life as a guitarist—or if she even continued playing at all.

The way I figured it, this note was written somewhere around 1995, and if Jessica had just been entering college, that would put her in her early thirties today.

Had GZ's pride been well placed? Had Jessica grown into the kind of adult he'd hoped she would? And why, if their relationship had been as special as the teacher's note implied, had Jessica gone on to sell this wonderful and sentimental gift? You'd think if she'd returned even a little of her teacher's affection, she'd at least have kept the note.

Given my sudden and intense curiosity about all this, I found myself faced with two possible paths: I could either make up imaginary answers to these questions, or I could snoop around to see if I couldn't uncover the real story of Jessica and GZ.

And I bet you can guess which road I traveled by.

Obviously, the name, Jessica, and the initials, GZ, weren't a whole lot to go on, so I did the only thing I could think of at the moment. Vintage guitars get bought, sold, and traded more often than the uninitiated might think. So it was unlikely, to say the least, that Jessica had just walked into the guitar shop and sold it to the proprietor. Nevertheless, I had to give it a shot. I called, asked for the owner of the store, and asked him if he could tell me the name of the guitar's previous owner.

"Sorry," he said. "I really can't help you with that."

"I understand," I said, disappointed. "You have to protect the confidentiality of your customers."

He laughed. "Yeah, I guess I do, but that's not what I mean. I bought it at a local guitar show from another dealer. There's no telling how many times that guitar's changed hands. As for tracking down who owned it last? Well, all I could tell you is good luck with that."

I thanked him and was just about to hang up when he asked me to hold on for a second.

"I don't know if this'll help you," he said. "But there was a guy in here the other day asking about that same guitar. Said he had a friend that used to have one just like it, and that he may be interested. But he hasn't come back yet."

My heart did a little zippity-zip. I wondered if that ever happened to the *Law and Order* guys when they got a lead. "You wouldn't happen to know his name, would you?"

"Dude," he said. "What kind of a salesperson do you think I am? Of course I took his name. Hold on . . ."

He left me hanging for a minute while I listened to him rustle through some papers.

"Here it is: Charles Roland."

"That's great," I said, and spelled the name back to him.

"And I bet you want his number, too, don't you?"

"I love you," I said.

I left a message on Charles Roland's voice mail. I told him briefly about the guitar and the note, and requested that if, by chance, he might know anything about any of this, that he please give me a call or drop me an e-mail. I left all my contact info and, not expecting any kind of response, figured that would be the end of the line for my fleeting life as a private investigator.

So, with my fantasy tucked neatly away with my guitar and the note folded in my shirt pocket, I decided to take a scenic drive up the coast and enjoy the impending sunset. I got in my car, headed up through La Jolla, and soon found myself entering the posh and charming little town of Del Mar. It had been a while since I'd stopped to fully take in the spectacle of the sun disappearing over the western horizon, so I decided to treat myself to a late-afternoon appetizer at Il Fornaio and watch Mother Nature's show from atop the Del Mar Plaza.

I parked the car in the lot and took the elevator to the open courtyard on the top floor, which offered a spectacular panoramic view of the blue water shining brilliantly in the light of the descending sun. I stepped up to the open-air bar at the restaurant, ordered calamari and a Diet Coke with lemon, and found an open table pushed up against the glass wind barrier.

I took a quick moment to scan the e-mail on my iPhone and saw that I had a recent message. My chest thumped when I read the subject line: "A response from Charles Roland." Polite and formal in his tone, Mr. Roland wrote that he was "surprised and delighted" to hear about that note and that, yes, he did know the people involved and would love to meet me so he could see it firsthand.

So, there it was. *Easy as pie,* I thought.

After a couple of terse, back-and-forth e-mails, we agreed to meet the next morning at a coffee shop in Pacific Beach, just a mile or so up Mission Boulevard from where I lived.

So, the following morning found me at Peet's Coffee, sitting at an outside table, and sipping a double shot mocha while I watched the early morning traffic. The ocean was just a block away and the salt smell was, thankfully, much stronger than that of the exhaust fumes. The marine layer fogged out the sunshine, and as the caffeine lifted the fog from my brain, I considered the meeting that was just about to take place. I was surprised at how excited I was to hear about Jessica and GZ. You'd almost think I didn't have any friends of my own.

"Good morning, Mr. Farber."

I looked up at, I assumed, Charles Roland.

"And you would be Charles Roland?" I said, rising politely from my chair.

"That I would," he said as we clasped hands.

Charles's appearance was unusual in that there wasn't anything unusual about his appearance. He was the kind of guy who'd easily blend in with the fortysomething suit-and-tie kind of crowd—not exactly the profile of the typical San Diego beach collection, but I figured that he was on his way to the office and was dressed for that world, not this.

He wore his dark brown hair in a conservative cut that gave the impression that he visited his barber every couple of weeks. His white shirt was starched and crisp and pressed in a way that, no matter what I did or had done to them, my shirts would never conform to. He wore a simple gold band on the ring finger of his left hand. With his gray suit and dark, patterned tie, I assumed Charles Roland must be some kind of a corporate stiff. An office drone in worsted wool.

Let me just say in my own defense that I am not a judgmental person by nature. I am, I would like to think, one of the more accepting people you'll ever meet, and I say that with utmost humility. In other words, my rush to judgment here was entirely out of character. Looking back on it now, I missed some of the more subtle signs of Charles Roland's demeanor, which, in retrospect, should have been as obvious as a tuba.

I offered to get him a coffee and he declined.

"So, Mr. Roland," I started in cautiously, "this is such a strange scenario. Kind of romantic in a way, isn't it?"

"I suppose so," he said, almost mechanically. "And please call me Charles. May I see the note?"

I handed it to him and watched him read. Except for a very slight rising of the eyebrows, his face was emotionless.

He handed the note back to me, saying nothing.

"So . . ." I just couldn't read this guy. "Jessica and GZ," I said into the awkward silence. "What can you tell me about them?"

"May I be blunt, Steve?" It must have been a rhetorical question, because he didn't wait for my answer. "I'm not so sure I am ready to do that."

That was the last thing I expected Charles Roland to say. "What do you mean?" I said, shocked. "I thought that's why you came to meet me."

"I said I'm not sure I'm ready yet. I didn't say no."

I waited for him to continue.

"I checked you out last night, Steve. Looked through your Web site, read some of your articles and an excerpt from one of your books. I think I have a pretty good sense of who you are—professionally, anyway."

"Okay. Good, I guess. But what's my work got to do with this?"

"You'll find it's got everything to do with it—that is, if you are who your materials claim you to be."

"Okay," I said, annoyed but still intrigued. "Why are you being so cryptic? Am I going to learn about these people or not?"

"My apologies, Mr. Farber, for being so vague. Here's the situation: For one thing, I'm very protective of the privacy of the individuals involved here—one of them, in particular, with whom I work. I'm sure you understand."

"Okay," I said.

"I don't want to waste their time with a . . . what . . . curiosity seeker. Any interaction with them needs to be . . . I guess I'd call it . . . meaningful for them."

"Meaningful," I repeated.

"Yes. But I believe there's a value in this for you, too, far beyond what you expected when you contacted me."

"Really," I said, more than a little skeptical now. "In what way?"

"I'm referring to a principle that made their relationship so special in the first place. Something was put in place between them that has developed into a philosophy of life that goes way beyond GZ, as you call him, and his young student. And given the kind of leadership work you do, it may be well worth your while to learn and understand the principle before you meet the people behind it. And, in fact, I've been authorized to say that neither one has any interest in sharing their story with you until and unless you grasp this principle first. Are you interested, Steve?" Again, he didn't wait for my answer. "Because if you are, I'm willing to teach you about it. And if you're not . . ."

"Uh-huh?" I asked, feeling pretty sure I knew what he was going to say.

"If not, we say good-bye right now. No harm; no foul, as they say."

He must have seen something in my face.

"Does that sound severe?" he asked.

"A little," I said. "Not to mention a touch bizarre."

"Perhaps," he said. "But I assure you that's the way they want it. That's the deal; take it or leave it."

I almost got up and left. I swear I came that close to bagging this whole thing—I mean, who did this Roland guy think he was? Who did he think I was, for that matter? I'm a busy guy, too, you know. He seemed to assume I had all this free time on my hands—that I had nothing better to do with myself. And who was he to teach me? Like I couldn't teach him a thing or two.

But as I worked through my indignant inner gyrations and calmed down a little, I was left with one clear, undeniable feeling: My heart was sinking at the thought of this story, this venture going up in a puff of my fragile ego.

"Okay," I said offhandedly. "I'm in. What do you call this life-changing 'principle' of yours? And it better not be *The Secret,* or we're done right now."

He sat up excitedly and clapped his hands together in an unexpected burst of energy.

"We call it Greater Than Yourself," he exclaimed, morphing from a virtual cadaver to an animated extrovert. "Or GTY, for short."

As soon as I'd said yes to his offer there was a near-instantaneous shift in Charles's personality—a new, comical energy in his voice, and enthusiasm on his face and in his gesticulating hands. His transformation threw me. Apparently, my initial snap judgment of Charles Roland, Company Zombie, had been way off.

"So, what happens next?" I managed to say.

"I," he said, wiggling his brows comically like Groucho Marx, "am taking you to school."

He fished a legal pad and pen from his leather Tumi briefcase and set them on the table in front of him.

"And me without my knickers and paste," I said. "What kind of school?"

"GTY School," said Charles. "And here's the agenda."

He held up three fingers on his left hand and ticked them off one at a time with the index finger of his right. "First, I give you an overview of the three tenets of GTY; second, we take a field trip to visit a practitioner and veritable guru on the subject; and, third, you do homework."

"Homework? Seriously?" I was never much of a fan.

"Yes. Tonight."

"But, *American Idol*'s on."

He ignored me. "And then if you pass the final and demonstrate worthiness by walking over hot coals, I'll take you to meet them."

The whole thing sounded overly dramatic and more than a little contrived, but Charles seemed eager to get on with it, so I just held my breath and jumped in.

"I'll take a pass on the blisters, but sign me up for the rest, I guess."

"A fine choice," he said, tearing off the wrinkled top page of the pad. "Shows excellent intellectual discrimination."

"Do you actually get paid for this, Charles?"

"And, why shouldn't I?" he said. He wrote *Greater Than Yourself* across the top of a clean, fresh page and turned the pad around to face me. "So," he said pointedly, "how about you cut the smart-ass shtick and help me earn my keep?"

There's nothing like starting out your first day of school with a good, hard spanking from the teacher.

"The basic and seemingly paradoxical truth of GTY is that truly great leaders in life," said Charles Roland, "become so because they cause others to be greater than themselves."

The words sounded familiar. "Who said that?" I asked Charles.

"Well, unless you're a ventriloquist, I did," he said mischievously.

On the surface, Greater Than Yourself was an inspiring tenet. But it also raised a whole boatload of questions. So I started with the obvious.

"Sounds like the Golden Rule, no?"

"Now that's a good place to start," said Charles, tilting his chair up on the back two legs. I never let my kids do that.

"Practically everyone knows Christianity's Golden Rule: 'Do unto others as you would have them do unto you,' whether they are Christian or not. Most of us have heard it since we were kids and have some version of it committed to memory. Somewhere in our hearts, subconscious, or wherever we store this kind of thing, we know that we're all supposed to practice what philosophers call the 'ethic of reciprocity.' "

A surprisingly scholarly dude, this Charles Roland, I thought.

"In fact," he exclaimed, "virtually every culture and school of thought on this planet—Christianity, Judaism, Islam, Hinduism, Buddhism, Humanism; spiritual, secular, philosophical, whatever—subscribes to some version of that same Rule. In principle, at any rate, we all seem to agree that this is a good thing."

"In principle," I said. "Practice is something else."

He leaned way back on his chair, holding on to the ridge of the table with his outstretched fingertips. "Of course. But even the principle gets muddy if you really pick it apart, so we're not going to do that. Let's just say that a whole lot of people from all walks of life agree—in principle—that human beings should do good for other human beings."

"Again," I said. "In *principle.*"

"Right," he agreed. "GTY is all about putting that into practice, Steve. It's about who we are and what we do, not what we say we should do."

"And you're going to show me how to do that."

"I want you to consider what would happen if you held yourself ridiculously accountable to the letter of the reciprocity principle," he said as he let his chair down on all fours and leaned across the table.

"And not just in your community service or volunteer endeavors, Steve, but in your day-to-day, get up and feed the kids, go to work, get yelled at, go for a run at lunchtime, come home, feed the kids, watch *American Idol,* go to bed, kinds of routines. Can you see yourself doing that?"

I didn't answer, but he didn't wait for me, anyway.

"And what if we all did? Wouldn't that be something?"

"Well, yeah," I said. "Of course it *would,* but . . ."

"Yes, it would! All of us practicing some version of the

Golden Rule throughout the day? Imagine how the customer service experience would change; imagine what our teams at work would be like; our companies' cultures; our families' dynamics. I mean really stop and imagine it—and it's pretty clear why the Golden Rule and its cousins have been an ideal through the ages and across the globe.

"Downright utopian, wouldn't you say?"

"Yes." I allowed myself the indulgence of imagining such a world. "I would say so."

"So pardon me for sounding insensitive and more than a little bit blunt, but it's not going to happen," he said sternly. "Not ever. Not on this planet."

"So what's your point?" I said.

" 'All of us' is just too idealistic an expectation. There are simply too many malcontents and miscreants out there, Steve, who will take a kind gesture and stuff it back down your throat."

"Speaking from experience, Charles?" I laughed at his ominous demeanor.

"The good news," he continued without answering, "is that changing the world doesn't require changing everybody in it. So let's forget about 'all of us' and focus on 'one of us.' "

Now I knew where he was heading with this.

"And that 'one of us' would be . . . ?"

He was getting too good at treating my questions as rhetorical.

"There are three tenets of Greater Than Yourself," said Charles, writing upside down on the pad so it was right side up to me. *"Expand Yourself, Give Yourself,* and *Replicate Yourself."*

I looked down at the pad as Charles looked intently at me. It was an intriguing idea. I wasn't sure how realistic it was, but I've always been somewhat of an idealist, so that didn't bother me too much. My concern at the moment, though, was a lot less lofty and far more practical.

"Before we get into this, Charles," I said, "how much school time are we talking about here, before I get to meet GZ and Jessica? I mean, is this going to take a day? A week? What?"

He put his pen on the table. "In other words, what do you have to do, and how long is this going to take, right?"

"Right."

"Well," he said, sinisterly rubbing his hands together, "as far as the 'what' part goes, all you have to do is satisfy me that you're ready to meet Jessica." He was having way too much fun with this mischievous mentor act, I thought. "And as for how long it'll take? That all depends on you."

"Oh, come on," I said, increasingly irritated. "Can I just get a straight answer, please?"

Apparently not. He ignored my snarkiness and tapped his pen on the pad of paper.

"The idea of Greater Than Yourself," he said, "is that it's

not your job to simply help, or to be a coach or a mentor—at least not in the ways most people do it. Your job is to do whatever you can, to act in such a way that you extend and offer yourself to another, with the expressed purpose of elevating that person above yourself.

"In other words, by the time you're 'done' working with them, so to speak, they will be greater at 'X' than you are. Are we clear on the intent here, Mr. Farber?"

"Clear," I said.

"Now," he continued, "if you're really going to take this seriously, to make others greater than yourself, you have to start the process not with them, but with yourself."

"Start with myself how?"

"Think about what has to be happening inside your head and heart. First, you have to have a very deep and expansive sense of who you are. Your self-confidence has to be unshakable and unwavering. You have to understand to the very core of your being that relationship is not a zero-sum game. Your heart has to be big enough to care about another's hopes and dreams at least as much as you care about your own. And you have to be getting better and better, more competent, smarter, more experienced, more connected to others all the time.

"Said another way," he said, circling the first point on the top of the pad, "you have to Expand Yourself before you can help make others greater."

"When you ain't got nothing, you got nothing to give," I said, massacring a classic Bob Dylan lyric.

"Once you have expanded yourself," he added, "you are ready for the next tenet of GTY."

"Give Yourself," I said, taking the pen from him and circling the second phrase on the page.

He laughed, leaned forward, and patted me on the shoulder. "You're a quick study.

"The old saw 'Knowledge is power' is absolutely true," he continued. "The problem is that most people—business people, anyway—interpret it to mean the *hoarding* of knowledge is power. If I have more knowledge than you, I win."

"Right," I said.

"Wrong," he replied. "The real payoff comes in the *giving* of knowledge, not the keeping of it. If I'm going to make you greater, I have to give freely of not only my knowledge, but all my resources: my connections and network, my experience, my insights, my advice and counsel—even my time."

"Be generous," I said. It was more of a question than a statement.

"More than generous," he said. "Give. It. All. Away."

I squirmed in my chair.

"Knowledge may be power, Steve, but the *giving* of knowledge and wisdom and experience and resources is far more powerful because it enriches both of us. You give to me and we both benefit."

"How do I benefit?" I challenged. "Because it feels good? Hey, I'm all for altruism, Charles, but that's not a compelling enough reason for me to give away everything I have. I've worked hard for it. And I'm—if I do say so myself—a fairly enlightened dude."

"Yes, you do say so yourself." He laughed. "And, you're right. It's not a good enough reason. The benefit for you is far, far greater than a warm, toasty feeling in your chest."

I waited for him to elaborate.

"If you earn a reputation, Steve, for being one who elevates others, for being someone who gives freely to those around him at work, for turning out superstars, what's going to happen? You'll have changed others' lives, but how will it change yours?"

But before I could reply, Charles forged ahead.

"I'll tell you how. Everyone will want to work with you. And, because of that, you'll be able to accomplish anything you set out to do.

"Whenever you want or need to get anything done—whenever you have an idea or venture that you want to pursue, people will come running to help. And for good reason: Aside from cashing in on all the priceless goodwill you've created, because of your track record everyone will know that by the time your project is completed, your idea implemented, your vision realized, they'll be all that much better off for having worked with you. Because you will have given them far more than they've given you. And so it goes, over and over again. Give more; get more. Give even more; get even more. Consider the possibilities, Steve. You'll see why hoarding your talents and yourself is eminently unproductive and—to be blunt—just plain stupid."

I'd never thought of it that way. And yet it made perfect sense. Envisioning the power of GTY kind of gave me goose bumps. I nodded my head slowly.

"It all circles back to a lovely little paradox: By focusing on making others greater than yourself, you become one of the greats, too. You join a fellowship of the rarest of all human beings."

"What fellowship is that?" I asked.

"The Creators of Masters," he said.

"The membership dues must be astronomical," I said.

Charles had already figured out that my irreverence was mostly just a put-on, so he allowed himself a perfunctory chuckle at my comment.

"But as great as that is," said Charles, "that's not where it stops."

"Something to do with this?" I asked, jabbing the pen on the last phrase, *Replicate Yourself.*

"Yes, it has everything to do with that," he said. "At the end of the day, it's simply not enough to make others greater than yourself."

"Why not?" I asked. "Sounds like a pretty good goal or legacy to me—Creator of Masters and all that."

"But it's not enough to accomplish the most important leadership act of all."

I knew exactly where he was headed with this, but I wanted to hear it from him.

"Which is?" I asked.

"To change the world," he said, as I'd known he would. "By making sure that the people you elevate are doing the same for others."

"Help them to 'pay it forward,' " I said.

"That's it precisely," said Charles. "Expand Yourself, Give Yourself, and, finally, Replicate Yourself by teaching others to do exactly what you've done for them."

"And that will eventually change the world?"

"I can't prove that," he said. "But there is one thing I will absolutely, unequivocally guarantee."

"What's that?"

"It sure couldn't hurt."

Charles gathered up his pen and pad and slid them into his briefcase. He pushed his chair back and stood. After smoothing his tie and buttoning the middle button of his suit jacket, he scooped up his belongings and walked toward the steps that led down to Mission Boulevard.

"Hey!" I called after him. "Where are you going?"

"Field trip!" he shouted without looking back. "Let's go! Time's a-wasting."

I stood up and followed Charles down to the street.

Let's hope not, I thought.

The brass, etched sign over the door said MAPLE TREE ENTERPRISES.

Charles and I had crossed Mission, walked over to the ocean-side boardwalk, and headed south about a quarter of a mile. In his expensive suit and tie, he'd looked so out of place among the skater/slacker/surfer beach crowd who populated this Pacific Beach neighborhood that I almost felt a little embarrassed for him. But if he'd been uncomfortable, he certainly didn't show it.

I didn't ask where we were going, and he never offered. After a couple of blocks, we'd cut left and then made a right down an alley running parallel to the water, which had led us to this door.

Charles knocked and rang the bell several times to no avail. So we walked back up the alley and around the front of the building, which faced the boardwalk and the ocean. I must have walked past this building hundreds of times over years of strolling up and down Mission and Pacific Beach, but I can't say I'd ever noticed it before.

It was a borderline dilapidated old house painted in faded shades of yellow and green, which stood in comical contrast to Charles's charcoal and white uniform. I guessed that Maple

Tree Enterprises—whatever that was—occupied the top half of the house, because the bottom porch of the house had been converted to an open-air bazaar, of sorts, which appeared to be a cross between a souvenir shop hawking T-shirts, sunglasses, postcards, and assorted San Diego trinkets, and a CD store with bins devoted to beach-indigenous genres like rock, grunge, punk, alternative, ska, and reggae.

Charles leaned against the seawall and, tilting his head back, raised two fingers to his mouth. He let loose with a trilled whistle that pierced my eardrums like a needle from a blowgun.

"Yow," I said.

He smiled at me, clearly proud of what a good whistler he was.

"Hey!" he called, shading his eyes as he looked up to the balcony overhead. "Plumeria! You in there?"

"What's a Plumeria?" I said, half to myself, half out loud.

"Well, hopefully," he said, pointing up, "Plumeria Maple, the one and only."

"The one and only what?" I said, a little too much out loud.

I looked up and saw the drapes rippling at the edges of the open sliding doors. Sure enough, moments later, Plumeria Maple, in all her glory, stood on the balcony above and beamed down at us with arms outstretched.

The phrase "in all her glory" is usually a euphemism—like "in her birthday suit" or the less subtle "nekkid as a plucked turkey," for example—but that's not how I use it here.

She was simply—and I don't use this word lightly—
glorious. All five-foot-ten, 220 pounds of her just radiated
congeniality. I found myself liking her instantly. She was in
her early sixties, I would have guessed, and her size was probably magnified by the bright, multicolored, flowered muumuu
that she wore. Judging by her white skin, rosy cheeks, and
pale blue eyes, I imagined that her wispy, bleached hair was
probably once naturally blond or strawberry. Her hands now
perched firmly on her hips and with her elbows jutting
sharply out to either side, she looked rather like a large floral-
patterned teapot as she stood there above us.

"Well, Chucky Roland," she called down. "Don't you look
all grown up in your Brooks Brothers jammies!"

"Hello, Maple," said Charles, unconsciously smoothing
down the front of his suit coat.

He smiled, but I detected a wince in his voice. He didn't
exactly like being called "Chucky," and yet there was a
smidge of fondness for it, nonetheless. At least, coming
from her.

"C'mon, Chucky." She laughed. "Someone's gotta let the
pressure out of that balloon head of yours."

"Yes. Well, thank you for that, Maple. I don't know what
I'd do without you."

"You'd float on up into space is what!" She chortled at
her own quip, a sister of the Smartass Society. Maybe that's
why I instinctually liked her.

"C'mon around back and I'll let you up—but only so I
can meet your friend here."

Charles shook his head as we walked back the way we'd
come.

"You know I love you, Chucky!" Plumeria Maple called after us.

He mumbled something under his breath, but his eyes were smiling, as I realized they had been since Ms. Maple made her appearance on the balcony.

This time the back door buzzed open. We entered and made our way up a flight of stairs to an open area on the top floor. It was sunny outside the sliding doors, but inside the room glowed with a light all its own. As my eyes focused, one impressive, high-end computer terminal after another came into focus. I soon saw that we were standing in the middle of a semicircle of half a dozen computer workstations. Their operators—three men and three women—faced toward the balcony and the ocean, with their backs to us.

A couple of them briefly spun in their chairs to check us out, and one gave a little wave over her shoulder. But for the most part we may as well have been a couple burps in the breeze for all the commotion our arrival caused.

Plumeria came around to us and embraced Charles in a hug that spoke volumes about the true feelings between them. I could sense that they'd known each other for a long time and shared a mutual warmth and affection. Charles then introduced us. Plumeria took my hand with both of hers and didn't let go as we exchanged the usual pleasantries. She beamed a smile reminiscent of the way I'd always pictured Mrs. Claus.

Still holding my hand, she led us out of the main room and into the master suite, which had been converted from a bedroom into a good-sized but moderately appointed office. A few comfortable chairs circled a small coffee table in one corner, and in the other, another impressive computer station sat atop a large maple (of course) desk.

Plumeria gestured us to sit and then walked around to her keyboard and tapped a few quick strokes.

"Just need to do . . . this!" Tap. "And . . . this!" Tap. "And . . . done! Now you've got my full attention, gentlemen," she exclaimed, walking over to sit with us. "Don't waste it."

I think it's fair to say we didn't.

While Plumeria Maple was clearly an interesting character, other than my assumption that this was supposed to be part of our GTY "field trip," I really didn't know why we were there. Charles didn't say a word; he seemed to be waiting for me to start the conversation.

"The *note*," Charles said, impatiently waggling his fingers. "Show her the note."

"Jeez," I said, obediently producing the piece of paper from my back pocket and handing it to Plumeria. "What am I, a mind reader?"

As she read, her expression gradually changed from curiosity to recognition. Then, as if suddenly understanding the full import of what she was reading, her face lit up like a beacon.

"Oh my," she exclaimed. "This is fabulous! Wonderful! Have you shown this to—"

"No," Charles abruptly cut in. "And before you say another word, Ms. Maple Mouth, let me explain our agenda here."

Charles went on to give an excellent overview of the events that had brought us to this moment and spelled out our agreement—that I wouldn't meet the people behind the note until I had successfully negotiated my GTY training. I marveled at his ability to summarize the relevant details and delete the unnecessary.

"So," Plumeria said to Charles, "I'm kind of like a guest lecturer, huh?"

I raised my hand, and she called on me.

"S'cuze me, Ms. Maple," I said, assuming the student role.

"How can I put this nicely?" I paused. "I really have no idea what this place is all about or—pardon me for saying so—who you are."

She looked accusingly at Charles, who shrugged guiltily.

"I like to be mysterious," he said.

"You know I love you, Chucky." Plumeria smiled, but I already recognized it as the first move in a one-two punch. "But smart as you are, sometimes you act like such a maroon."

Looking back at me, she said, "C'mon. Let me show you around."

We walked into the main room and she made quick introductions of the folks sitting around the semicircle of workstations, who were polite and rather charming in a geeklike sort of way as they glanced up briefly from their screens to say hello.

"Geniuses," she said to me, shaking her head in awe. "Every single one."

"Got that right," said the guy on the end.

"Maple Tree Enterprises," Plumeria explained, blowing Genius a kiss, "is an under-the-radar player in the Internet and social networking world. You haven't heard of our company, but you'd certainly know some of the Web sites and blogs that we developed and run." She named a few of them. Even to me, not the savviest guy in the blogosphere, it was a wildly impressive list. I recognized one social networking site as a serious up-and-comer; another had already become nearly ubiquitous in the corporate world.

"We also create customized e-learning intranet sites for Fortune 500 clients."

"In short," Charles interjected, sweeping his arm in a dramatic gesture, "Maple Tree Enterprises is an Internet behemoth, wrapped up in a quaint, unassuming package."

"Holy cannoli," I said, eloquent as usual.

"But what my dear friend here won't tell you about herself," Charles continued, "is that she sits on the boards of at least a half-dozen nonprofit and charitable organizations."

Plumeria modestly tried to wave him off, but Charles disregarded her.

"She's a philanthropist in the truest sense of the word," he said, "and her reluctance to admit it is just further evidence of this woman's amazing heart."

"Hear, hear," said Genius, never looking up from his screen.

A deep blush spread over Plumeria Maple's face like a sunset reflecting off the snow.

"Well, okay then," I said to Charles. "Now that I feel wholly inadequate, what is this all about?"

"Well," Charles said, talking more to Plumeria than to me, "I thought that Maple could give you her perspective on the Greater Than Yourself philosophy. She's as inspiring and adept a practitioner as you'll ever find."

"And you know those people in the note," I said, hoping to lead her into naming names.

"Oh, yes. Dear, dear friends, in fact. And you at least know *of* one of them, too. She's quite a success . . ."

"Whoa, Maple!" Charles quacked. "Lesson first; people later. Maybe."

"All right, Chucky!" she quacked back. "Don't get your Calvins in a clod."

Plumeria put her arm around my shoulders and walked me back into her office.

"Greater Than Yourself, Steve," she said as we walked, "is not an idea to be taken lightly."

"Clearly not," I said.

She stopped and looked me squarely in the face. "I mean it. This is way too important to give lip service to."

"I understand," I said.

"Do you? Really?"

I paused, unsure of where she was headed with this.

"Pardon me for saying so, Steve. But aren't you in the lip-service business?"

"Excuse me?" She'd asked the question so sweetly that I was blindsided by the connotation. "Are you saying I'm a con artist?"

"No. I'm *asking* you if you are. You speak, and write books, right?"

"Right. Basically."

"Well, that's not going to be enough anymore."

"It's not like I don't do other things," I said, feeling myself growing uncomfortably defensive.

"No, that's not what I'm saying. I'm saying that writing and speaking and whatever else you've done so far won't be enough in the future. I'm saying that if you want to explore the principles of Greater Than Yourself, you have to commit to the practice of it."

She stopped, looked over at Charles, and then back to me.

"You're going to have to make me a promise, Steve. A vow."

"A vow?" I asked, resisting the temptation to crack a joke to lighten the mood.

"That you will never speak or write on this subject in your talks and books unless you're doing it yourself."

Now, I've been in the leadership development field for nearly two decades. I've taught countless workshops to hot-shot executives on how to become a better leader. And no one—not once—has dared me not to teach unless I dared to do.

And yet it made all the sense in the world.

So I raised my right hand. "Sign me up," I said.

"Consider yourself vowed," she said, escorting me over to the chair next to her office workstation.

Frankly, I'm usually reluctant to sign on the dotted line, metaphorically speaking, but in this case I really didn't think taking a pledge would be a big deal. And if for some unforeseen reason GTY turned out to be over my head or too far outside of my comfort zone, I just wouldn't talk or write about it. So, yes, I'd taken a vow, but, no, I wasn't completely committed. It wasn't *serious*.

I was wrong, of course.

"Now, first things first: Do you have your checkbook with you, Steve?"

"My checkbook?"

"Yes. You know, that little folder the bank gives you that allows you access to your money."

A wild clamoring of alarm bells went off in my head. Was she about to hit me up for cash?

"Yeah. I know what a checkbook is."

It's remarkable how fast the mind works. They say that your entire life flashes by when you're about to die, and I believe it—at least I believe that it's possible for the mind to react that way, because in less than a nanosecond my brain jammed the events of the previous twenty-four hours into rewind.

I'd found the note, connected with Charles, and followed him here. But what did I really know about these people?

Nothing. Zip.

I'm a trusting person—too trusting, some would say. I never checked out Charles Roland; I just took him at face value and jumped on for the ride. The guy at the guitar shop knew him, but in what capacity? Probably none other than what's required for a basic customer transaction.

And Plumeria Maple? How come I'd never heard of a woman ostensibly so influential in the online tech world? And here she is asking me for money? Something was very wrong.

"Why would I need my checkbook?" My eyes darted to the door and back to her.

"If you would, please," Plumeria said, a little too sweetly. "Make a check out to the Maple Trust for . . ."

I waited, playing along for the moment, but having no intention of writing anything in any amount.

". . . now I'm assuming you wouldn't keep the full quarter million in your checking account. . . ."

"The full what?"

". . . so let's start today with the five-thousand-dollar initial donation."

I stared blankly at her.

"Chucky! You didn't tell him about this, either?"

There was that Charles Roland shrug again.

"I'm so sorry, Steve," she said, as sincere as can be. "Looks like I've taken you by surprise, thanks to little Chucky here. So, I'll tell you what. Let's start with whatever you have in your account today, and we'll work up to the rest of the five K later."

"No," I said, gathering my thoughts. "I'll tell *you* what." My voice rose as I stood up. "I don't know what kind of scam you two are running, or just how stupid you think I am, but I'm not 'donating' jack to you people."

As I walked toward the door, Charles jumped up and blocked my way.

"I think," said Charles, too calmly for the situation, "that you should hear the nice lady out."

I couldn't believe this. "What's wrong with you? Do you think you can force me to pay?"

"I shouldn't have to," said Chucky. "Because unless I'm mistaken," he nearly whispered, "a couple of minutes ago you took a vow."

"I vowed to practice GTY before I talk about it. What's that got to do with writing a check?"

"Let me put it this way," he said, now smiling. "You've been punked."

It was a bit of a mystery how I could feel so relieved and so stupid at the same time. Charles and Plumeria broke into raucous peals of laughter.

"Ho, Chucky! That was good! *You should hear the nice lady out,*" she mimicked, slapping him on the back. "Chucky the Wiseguy! I love it!"

Charles was laughing so hard his eyes were tearing. "Yeah, and you, Maple! *I assume you don't have the full quarter million.* I thought he was going to have a stroke right there on the spot!"

"Oh, we are good," crowed Plumeria. "We. Are. *Good.*"

They high-fived each other.

"I'm still here," I said.

"Sorry, Steve. Sorry, sorry." Plumeria wiped her eyes with the sleeve of her muumuu. "Please, sit down and let me explain. Come. Let's talk."

I allowed myself a small chuckle at my own expense, although I still had no idea what the joke was all about, except that somehow it was on me. The three of us sat down around the small coffee table.

"I just wanted to give you that visceral sense of what it feels like when you think someone is trying to get their hands on your limited resources. You thought I was trying to take advantage of you, so you bristled. I mean, that's your hard-earned money in that bank. You weren't about to give it over to someone you'd just met just because she asked you to. You were convinced that you were being played."

"Well, of course I bristled," I said. "You would've, too."

"Sure. No doubt about it." She closed her eyes briefly.

"But what if"—she continued tentatively—"what if you had a billion dollars in that account? Would you have reacted differently?"

I thought about it. "I'm not really sure. I might have been more amused than threatened, I guess. But even a billionaire wouldn't just fork over that kind of cash."

"But," Charles interjected, "would you have been more likely to hear us out?"

"Not if it happened this way!"

"How then?"

"If I trusted you and liked you, sure, I'd want to hear you out. In fact, I might even approach you to find out what you're up to."

"Yes," said Plumeria. "Trust. Relationship. All that good, human stuff. Nothing will flow unless there is trust present between people.

"But now," she said, pointing her finger at me, "take this to the next step, Mr. Billionaire. Let's say you listened to my proposition—whatever it was—and you decided that it was a great, grand idea with a lot of promise. Not only did you believe in the idea, but you believed in me and in my ability to carry it out. What would you do? Remember—you're a billionaire now."

"I'd do a lot more than write a check, most likely," I said.

"Like what?"

"Well, if I have that kind of money, I must know lots of influential people in business and politics." I was enjoying this fantasy. "And I would want to connect you with the right ones."

"So you're going to give more than your money," she re-iterated.

"Yeah. And I'd want a seat on your board."

"Done!" Plumeria said, reaching out her hand. I shook it.

"Now, all I'll need is that billion dollars." I laughed.

"Ahhh!" exclaimed Charles. "That's just the point, isn't it?"

"What is?"

"The greater your resources, the more help you can give," Plumeria said. "Now, forget about the billion *dollars*. This isn't about money, you see. Think of the money as a metaphor for all the *other* resources you have, the really vital ones: your talent, your knowledge, your connections, your confidence, your trust, and your time—all of it. Those are your resources, Steve. And I'll bet if you think of it that way, you're a lot closer to being a billionaire than you realized moments ago."

"Maybe," I said.

"Now, here's the point," Plumeria continued. "Did Chucky tell you about the second tenet of GTY?"

"Yes," I fumbled. "It's . . . um . . . Give Yourself?"

"Right. So, riddle me this: How are you going to Give Yourself if your 'account' is empty?"

"Or," said Charles, "think of it like this: In order to Give Yourself in a significant way to another's progress and expansion . . ."

"You have to Expand Yourself first," said Plumeria, finishing Charles's sentence. "Self-expansion is a perpetual enterprise. And because it's the foundation of whatever you do for others, expanding yourself is the furthest thing from selfishness. You expand yourself in order to give yourself to others."

"I like the sound of that," I said, breathing in deeply. "But it's easier said than done, isn't it?"

"Most good things are." Plumeria Maple sighed. "But we have one tremendous advantage: We human beings are expansive by nature. We're driven by an innate desire to continually prove to ourselves the vastness of our influence and interconnection. Your influence on others is so much bigger, Steve, than your body and brain sitting here in these few square feet in this room in this neighborhood in San Diego. Your boundaries are, literally, limitless."

She was starting to push the needle on the hooga-booga meter. "You mean expanded consciousness and all that stuff. With all due respect, Plumeria, that's a philosophical point that we could debate for a lifetime."

"Well, that would be stimulating, I'm sure. But philosophy doesn't pay the bills around here, my friend. In fact, forget philosophy for a moment, Steve, and just consider the technology."

She spread her arms out to indicate her workplace.

"This entire business, and many, many more like it, is built on the very principle of Expand Yourself—on our desire to be bigger tomorrow than we are today. Social networking, the blogosphere, all that new and soon-to-come technology is enabling us to experience more of our true nature: We want to stretch around the world and connect to more and more people, no matter where we are *physically*.

"For example, mobile networking is essentially a little teensy baby today, but it's expected to be a six-billion-dollar industry by 2012. And that's going to seem like nothing by the time 2020 comes along—mark my words. And that's not even considering the technology that hasn't been thought up yet. Eventually, when this kind of technology spreads to every populated nook and cranny on the planet—and it will—you will literally have the capability to connect with every single human being on Earth."

I wasn't an expert by any means, but having started to dabble in my own blog a couple of years earlier, I did know my way around the Web a little bit. And there's no doubt that the number of people in my life I count as friends—and I mean real friends, not the kind you click to become—had grown significantly through the experience. But, still and all, I'd never thought about it the way Plumeria had just laid it out.

I all but buzzed at what seemed to me a profound, new perspective. Plumeria guessed accurately at the meaning behind the expression on my face.

"There you go, Steve. You're getting a taste of the first element of Expand Yourself. Simply put, you're not the lonely little guy you thought you were; you're only as solitary as you choose to be. And that, in fact, is the first element of Expand Yourself: *Shift your perspective* from isolated to connected; from alone to interdependent; from me to us.

"After all, even if the old saying is true that we come into and go out of this world alone, it's just tragically selfish if we act as though it applies to all the time in between. Ultimately, it comes around to this perspective, Steve: In whatever roles we play in life (and we all play many)—leader, citizen, employee, executive, parent, spouse, friend, elected official—our job is not to hoard but to help."

"And from there," said Charles, stretching his legs out in front of him, "everything else is just cream cheese."

Plumeria picked up a yellow legal pad from her desk and tossed it along with a pen in my direction. It landed with a *thwap* on the coffee table in front of me.

Before I could react, she held up her index finger as if to say, "Just a minute," and called out through her office door in the direction of the geek pen.

"Hey, Genius!" she bellowed. "Come in here for a minute, would you please?"

After a brief pause, the kid who'd been sitting at the end of the semicircle sauntered into the room, hands in the pockets of his cargo shorts. I loved the way his look and demeanor exuded the stereotypical mien of the young, precocious techno-geek. Round, wire-framed glasses, Einstein-like black hair jutting in all directions, and a hint of light acne trailing across his forehead. He leaned in the doorway with a bemused smile on his face. He didn't look more than eighteen or nineteen years old.

"Your Majesty?" he said.

"In, in, in," she said. "Sit for a minute."

Bowing in mock subservience all the way, he walked over and sat down next to me.

We shook hands and he introduced himself to me as Jim Hack.

"Hack?" I said, not sure I'd heard him correctly.

"Yeah, yeah, I know." He rolled his eyes. "Way too obvious a handle for someone in my line of work. Not my fault."

"Genius here just turned twenty-one," said Plumeria, standing again teapot-style in front of us. "My first employee. He was a senior in high school when he hired himself here exactly four years ago this week. He comes in when he can between school and studying. Gets more work done than anyone, though."

"Where you going to school?"

"UCSD. Majoring in computer science," he said, adding more grist to the name-taunting mill.

"With a specialization in bioinformatics," added Charles. "Whatever that means."

"Impressive," I said. Then, my brain registered something I'd heard a moment before.

"Wait," I said to no one in particular. "He hired himself? What does that mean?"

"It means she wasn't looking to hire me or anyone," answered Jim. "She was just a nice, rich lady happy to spend her time overseeing her family trust, serving on nonprofit boards and donating money to causes she believed in. I was the one that infected her with the entrepreneurial bug. I had this idea for an information business and I came in one day and pitched her on it."

"He was just so smart." Plumeria laughed. "I never even said yes. He just showed up again the next day with his laptop and started doing stuff that I didn't even understand at first. Never left since."

"You hired yourself," I said.

"Yep. But then Plumeria started to challenge me. She said, 'Okay, if you're gonna do something, do something great.' She told me to figure out what kind of talent I needed and then start building a team.

" 'Hire more people,' she told me. 'And if they're not better or smarter than you when you hire them, it'll be your responsibility to make sure they get there.' I had no freaking idea what she was talking about at the time, but I tried anyway.

"And, now, every one of those five people out there"—Jim waved his hand toward the door—"makes me look like a dweeb."

"GTY," I said, assuming he knew what that meant.

"When Her Majesty told me my job was to make the people on my team greater than myself," continued Jim, "I really squirmed. It made me very, very uncomfortable."

Of course, I thought. *That's because you were probably an arrogant, self-absorbed teenager who always thought that he was the smartest guy in the room.*

"Why?" I said out loud, convinced I already knew the answer. Wrong again.

"Because I just didn't see what I could possibly have to give. I was a kid. In high school. I had virtually no experience working with others. People looked at my creativity and technical skills and saw me as having tons of confidence; but inside, my self-image had *mondo-geek* stamped all over it. The only reason I had a date to prom was because my best friend's stepsister didn't. I really didn't see myself as valuable, so the proposition of *giving myself* seemed worthless."

I jabbed my thumb in the direction of his team. "You obviously got past that, right?"

"In large part, yeah."

"How'd you do it?"

"Well, honestly, I'm still working on it. But I figure it this way: In order for me to be able to give to my team and my clients—to anyone, for that matter—I have to work really hard at expanding my knowledge, skills, and experience. That's why I'm going to a great school and studying my rear off.

"I always wanted to do that, anyway." Jim looked at Plumeria and smiled. "But she helped me see a new, deeper reason why it was so important. She gave me a new context: I needed to get better and better so I would have more and more to give away.

"That's very clear to me now, but back in the beginning, back when I started hiring people, I first had to acknowledge that I already *had* a lot to give. Much more than I'd given myself credit for."

"First thing I had him do," said Plumeria, "was take inventory."

"Of what?" I asked.

Jim Hack stood up and quickly excused himself in a way that gave me the distinct impression that he didn't want to bear witness to what was coming next. Plumeria took his place in the seat next to me and slid the pad and pen within my reach on the coffee table. Suspecting I knew what she wanted, I picked them up without being asked, placed the pad on my lap, and fidgeted the pen with my right hand.

"Your primary job," she said, "is to make sure that your own, personal inventory is constantly expanding. You are a storehouse with no walls and no ceiling. No matter how smart you get, no matter how many times you travel the world, no matter how many great people you think you know, you can always learn more, you can always experience more, you can always connect more and love more. That's the great and mysterious thing about human beings.

"Unfortunately, though, few people pay attention to their inventory. They don't know what they have, or, worse, they assume they have nothing; therefore, the very idea of giving to others feels threatening. Depleting. And that can be a terrifying experience, because a fully depleted person is . . . what?"

"Empty," I said.

"Dead," she countered. "On an unconscious, primal level some people are afraid to give to others because it feels like they're killing themselves in the process."

I'd never heard it expressed like that before. It made an awful lot of sense and explained much of the selfish behavior that I'd seen in my life—particularly in the corporate world. It was sobering.

"So, first thing is to recognize what you have, then take personal accountability for increasing it every waking hour of every day of your life. Make sense?" She waited for me to respond.

"Yes. Perfect sense," I said.

"Alright, then. Time for you to take inventory, don't you think?"

No surprising punch line there. "So, what do I do?"

"Simple," she said. "Make a list."

"Of what?" I asked again.

"Of all the valuable things contained within the storehouse called Farber."

I felt a kind of trembling similar, I was sure, to what Jim had described.

"I'm not sure I like the way this feels," I said meekly. She waited for me to elaborate.

"Maybe because it seems kind of arrogant to write a long list—to puff myself up like that."

"Or?" She rolled her hands in the air.

"Or . . . maybe because I'm afraid I won't have much of a list at all."

"Either way," said Charles, choosing to chime in on the conversation, "you'll get used to it, I promise. Just give it a whirl."

"How do I start?" I was procrastinating, I admit. But I'm glad I asked because Plumeria's next bit of guidance helped quite a lot.

"There's really no hard science to it," she said. "But you may find it easier to categorize in some way; for example, one category may be *Things I Do Well,* and another, *Meaningful Experiences I've Had,* or *Lessons I've Learned.* Another category might be *People I Know.* And so on."

"How about *Places I Know to Run Away and Hide In,*" I said out of the corner of my mouth.

Charles laughed. "One category you would do well with is *Techniques for Delaying Uncomfortable Self-Analysis.* I bet you can fill up a whole pad with that."

"Very funny," I said.

And then, slowly at first, I began to write.

They sat in silence and waited while I struggled away at my list for a good ten minutes. And then, mercifully, Plumeria suggested that I stop for a while, reflect on it, and come back to it later in the day when I had some free time. I'd written a few things about my experience as a speaker and writer, and some more with what I saw as the qualities of my character. For example, I had written "loyal friend" near the top of my list. That wasn't very specific, so I reminded myself to revisit and expand on that one later on. *Homework,* I thought.

Plumeria didn't ask to see the list, and I never offered, but she did have something to say about what I should do with it.

"This is not a drill," she said. "It is not an exercise that I had you do in order to make a point. This is a practice that should become part of your life. Integrate it into your thought process and into the way you make decisions. Will doing X add to your inventory? Will it expand an item that's already there? If so, do it; if not, don't.

"And then, every so often—maybe once a quarter, you decide—take another inventory. Every time you do it, you should find it to be larger and richer than the last one. Every time.

"Because you'll have shifted your perspective from hoarding to helping, you'll better understand that the whole purpose for growing your inventory, the ultimate mission behind your personal expansion, is to give it all away."

"Which is in reality a misnomer," said Charles as he yawned and stretched. "*Giving* implies a credit/debit balance sheet, but that doesn't apply here. No subtraction ever takes place. Not really. It only feels that way to the shortsighted."

"So, there you go, my new friend," said Plumeria as she stood and walked back to her computer. "Expand Yourself by shifting your perspective from isolation to connection, and by growing your inventory day in and day out.

"There's always more to it, of course, but that's a fine start, wouldn't you say?"

I would.

"Just one more thing," she said as she typed away on her keyboard. "As you're putting all this into practice—which, let me remind you, you have vowed to do—ask yourself about your legacy."

"My legacy?" Legacy had become a popular idea in the management consultant circles—we were always encouraging senior executives to think about theirs, but I wasn't anywhere near retirement age.

"Hey, if I had it my way," she said, reading my mind, "*children* would be encouraged to think about their legacy from the moment they start thinking about what to be when they grow up. This has nothing to do with how old you are; it has everything to do with what kind of person you want to be every day of your life.

"I wish everyone's legacy had one thing in common: to be

remembered long after they're gone as a person who made others' lives better."

"Can't really argue with that," I said.

"Alright," said Plumeria. "Then commit to it. Start your Greater Than Yourself legacy right now."

Inadvertently, I gulped.

"Don't worry—I'm going to make it easy for you. Great, lasting legacies are built one brick at a time. All I want you to do, Steve"—she was looking at her computer screen and fiddling with the mouse on her desk—"is to pick one person, and make that one person your own, personal GTY project. Raise that person, boost him or her above yourself. Start there and see what happens. Is that too much to ask?"

Frankly, I wasn't sure how to answer that. I wasn't sure how to begin making someone else my personal project. But I would have felt like too much of a wuss to bow out now.

"Good!" she said, assuming my silence meant acquiescence. "But be sure to choose that person wisely. Pick someone that you trust, someone that you fully, deeply believe in.

"Now"—she raised her head and looked at me—"I have something for you."

Charles and I looked at each other—it seemed like he had no idea what she was talking about, either.

"I've just registered, in your name, the Web address GreaterThanYourself.com. It's yours to do with what you will."

Now that was an unusual gift—one I had no idea what to do with. It was kind of like a modern-day version of soap-on-a-rope. Or fruitcake. Or fruitcake-on-a-rope. Even so, no one had ever given me a domain name before.

"Um, thank you," I said.

She laughed at my tepidity. "You'll figure out how to use it, I'm sure."

"Maple," said Charles, rising and motioning me to do the same. "It's been a pleasure, as usual."

"Yes," I agreed. "Thanks so much for taking the time with me. I've learned a lot."

"Damned with faint praise," she chuckled, even though I really did mean it. "Anytime, my new friend. Anytime, indeed."

She escorted us through the office and we said our good-byes to Jim and his team. As we reached the door that we'd come through a short time ago, Plumeria put her hand on my shoulder.

"And by the way," she said softly, "thanks so much for sharing Gene Zander's note. I'm so glad it was you who found it, and that it led you to me. I love it when life presents us with such wonderful, serendipitous connections."

"Gene Zander?" I said as Charles smacked himself on the forehead.

"Oops," said Plumeria Maple.

Supposedly, your ears burn when someone, somewhere is talking about you. It makes me wonder what's supposed to burn when you're being Googled.

Whatever it is, that must have been what Gene Zander experienced that morning, because as soon as I returned home from Maple Tree Enterprises, I'd wasted no time in firing up my laptop and typing his name into the ubiquitous search engine.

Gene Zander, Rancho Santa Fe, was not only a retired music teacher, he was also a former hotshot insurance executive—and a bit of an industry legend, at that. I found an old write-up about his retirement party that described how he'd gotten up to give a thank-you-and-farewell speech and, instead, played an instrumental rendition of the Beatles' "Long and Winding Road" on his guitar. And while he'd left the insurance life behind, it looked like he was still taking on a few guitar students. I found a listing for his studio in Rancho Santa Fe and called the number.

Zander answered the phone after a couple of rings. I introduced myself and explained why I was calling. After reading him the note, I asked if I could drop by to show him the guitar. He agreed, and before you could say, "blast from the past," I was out the door and on my way to his studio.

I strapped the guitar into its rightful place in the passenger seat (I couldn't bring myself to throw it in the trunk like so much luggage) and drove north up the 5 freeway. Rancho Santa Fe is a small, affluent town a few miles inland from the San Diego coast. Although I hadn't spent much time there, I always loved the upscale, Spanish feel of the place. Gene Zander's studio was on the second floor of a building across from Delicias restaurant. As I got to the top of the stairs, I heard the strains of a screaming guitar lick coming from behind the doors of suite number 3. There was no sign on the door, but it was pretty obvious I was in the right place, so I knocked just below the number and waited for the music to stop.

After a couple of beats of silence, the door swung open and I found myself looking down at the top of a shiny bald head, which, I guessed, belonged to the shorter-than-expected maestro. He pushed me aside with his arm, poked his head out into the open hallway, looked hastily right and left, and then pulled me into the room, clenching my arm as though I would try to escape.

"Are you being followed?" he whispered urgently. He looked up at me and then eyed my guitar case with great intensity.

I thought he was kidding, putting on some kind of a show, so I played along.

"I didn't see anyone," I whispered back. "Should I have?"

"Your hair's too long," he said.

"My hair?"

He looked into my eyes as a look of deep concern spread over his doughy face. "Don't feed the mullet," he urged.

"The what?"

"The mullet. Don't. Feed. The. Mullet."

And then I realized something that hadn't even vaguely occurred to me when I'd talked to him briefly on the phone.

Gene Zander, master guitarist and teacher, retired executive vice president of a Fortune 500 company, wasn't kidding at all.

He was—to put it simply—crazy as a loon.

He took the case gingerly from my hand and gestured for me to follow. We walked down the hall and turned left into a room toward the back of the unit. My heart stopped as I found myself standing in the middle of rack after rack of magnificent guitars. This was a collector's collection, the kind that every guitarist only dreams of owning: Martins, Fenders, Gibsons, Collings, Taylors, acoustic and electric, vintage and new. I looked anew at the twitchy and diminutive Mr. Zander and tried to reconsider my judgment of "crazy." You'd have to have pretty good access to most of your mental faculties to amass and care for an arsenal like this, it seemed to me. As I squinted at the strange little man, I felt a sudden tap on the back of my shoulder. Startled, I spun around with a gasp.

"Steve," said a significantly taller, gray-haired man, "I'm Gene Zander." He gave my hand a firm, professional squeeze. "Cal," he said to the short guy, "thanks for showing Mr. Farber in. You can finish watching your show if you'd like."

From the way Cal shoved the case back into my hands and shot out of the room, it appeared that he'd been watching a favorite. It took me a moment to regain my equilibrium.

"I'm sorry, Mr. Zander," I stammered.

"Gene," he said.

"Gene. I assumed he was you."

"He does kind of look like me." Gene laughed, mercifully interrupting me. "And it's not surprising, since he's my older brother.

"Cal has a few challenges, as you may have noticed. The sixties didn't leave him entirely intact. Cal was always adventurous, but he went on a few too many . . . adventures . . . and has never completely returned."

"Got it," I said.

"When I retired from the company, I moved him in with me. After all, I do love him like, well, a brother." He smiled.

For the first time I allowed myself to really look at Gene Zander. He was a man who all but oozed charisma. In fact, Gene Zander was quite possibly the best-looking man for his age I'd ever seen. He stood around five foot nine or ten. He seemed incredibly fit—as in two hundred crunches without breaking a sweat sort of fit. He wore his gray hair long and wavy in a way that reminded me of paintings I'd seen of Beethoven. I guessed he was around sixty years old, but he looked much younger.

"May I have a look at that guitar?" he said, motioning me over to a couple of chairs on either side of a killer 1965 Fender Twin Reverb amplifier.

I set the case down, lifted the lid, and handed my prize to Gene, which he accepted with great care.

"Yes. This is it," he said, his eyes misting. "Jessica sold it during a financially rough patch as a starving student in her junior year at San Diego State. She called me crying after she'd done it, afraid that I'd never forgive her." He strummed a few chords.

"Did you?" I asked, dying to know who Jessica was.

"There was nothing to forgive. She needed the money; she was a starving student. And as tasty as this guitar is, you can't eat it, can you?"

I marveled at the love and compassion Zander obviously still had for his former student. "Would you mind telling me about her?"

"Well, let's just say that Miss Jessica's not starving anymore." He smiled and plugged a tweed patch cord into the guitar's jack. "And now . . ." He powered on the amp, flipped a couple of switches, turned a few knobs, and paused. "Let's see how this old gal's held up in the hands of strangers."

I could easily compare Gene Zander's guitar playing to masters like Clapton, B.B., and Buddy Guy—certainly his technical and artistic skill and taste were on par with them—but I won't, because Gene had a style all his own. He didn't have super-fast chops, but they were melodic and fluid—there seemed to be virtually no emotional distance between what he felt in his heart and what came out through his fingertips. I had never heard anyone play that well in so close and personal a setting, and I was dumbstruck.

We passed the guitar back and forth a couple of times over the next hour, which was intimidating for me at first. I soon saw, however, what made Gene such an extraordinary teacher: When it was my turn, he encouraged me, guided and urged me on, and made me feel that I could play at least as well as he someday. I was hoping for an invitation to explore the racks of instruments that hung all around us. I'd have to wait for that, though.

Suddenly—it was as though the meter had run out of time—Gene placed the old Gibson back in the case and snapped the latches shut.

"Thank you," he said, "for bringing back some great memories. Jessica was a special kid, and now she's a special and successful woman. I am—just as I wrote in that note many years ago—very, very proud of her and what she's accomplished in life." He stood up in a way that suggested our meeting was over.

His sudden departure behavior took me by surprise, and I wasn't nearly ready to leave. Acting quickly, I pulled the note from my shirt pocket and held it up.

"Don't you want to look at this?" I offered.

He took it from me tentatively, his eyes misting again as he glanced over his handwriting from so long ago.

"Did she ever become a professional musician?" I asked, hoping to coax a few details from him.

"Oh, she could have been, that's for sure." He smiled wistfully. "She could hold her own with the best of the best. But, no, she's not a working musician. She took a different path altogether."

"You're still in touch with her?"

"Every now and then we touch base. And once in a while—maybe once a year—we get together and play a little." He paused. "When we do, it's the highlight of my year."

I had a question I wanted to ask, one that was a little delicate. I didn't know if I'd earned the right to ask it. But there was only one way to find out.

"Gene, it sounds like you two had—still have—a very special relationship together?"

"Yes. It's the wonderful thing about teaching. Every so often a student becomes part of you—much like what a parent feels for a child—and that bond never fades."

"So, why, do you think"—I chose my words carefully—"she left the note in the case when she sold the guitar?" I was thinking, she may have had to sell the instrument, but you'd think she would have kept that little piece of paper forever. Since the moment I'd found the note, I couldn't help but wonder if things between the two of them had been as rosy as Gene's words had depicted them. Maybe there was a reason Jessica didn't want to remember her teacher.

"My guess is she never found it." He ran his callused fingertips over the note, bemused. "I hid it under the lining as a surprise. I was sure that it would eventually worm its way out, or that she would ultimately discover it—that one day, somewhere down the road, it would appear and give an unexpected boost to her day." His smile was plaintive. "Looks like Cat never even knew it was there."

Could I be the one to deliver the note to her? I thought. What a wonderful moment that would be, to deliver Gene's words of encouragement from so long ago. That unexpected boost to her day could take place, after all.

Wait a minute, I thought. *What did he just say?*

"*Who* never knew?" I blurted.

Gene stopped short, suddenly. His face turned pale, and then went bright red.

"I said Jessica never knew," he stammered.

"You didn't say Jessica; you said Cat."

"Did I? I don't know why I would have said that . . ." His voice trailed off.

"That's what I heard," I said, refusing to let it go.

He sighed at last. "Yes, you're right. I did," he admitted. "Her friends started calling her Cat in college, and it stuck. Very few people even know her real name anymore."

And just like that, it all clicked. I had read about Cat in

the local and national business rags. A couple of the more personal profiles mentioned her lifelong interest in music— guitar music, to be exact. And that quote from Charles about causing others to be great? I remembered now where I'd read it: an *Inc.* magazine article about YSC Corporation and its CEO, Cat Cassidy.

Suddenly it all made perfect sense: Gene's student, Jessica, had grown up to become Cat Cassidy, the colorful, young renegade CEO of San Diego–based YSC Corporation—a dominant player in the staffing industry and one of the fastest-growing privately held companies in the country.

Gene's student had become a kind of rock star after all.

And I was the proud owner of what once had been the young Miss Cassidy's axe.

"Gene," I said, filled with the excitement of this new discovery, "could I ask you a favor?"

I took his silence as permission to continue. I explained what I do professionally, and why I'd been interested in the story behind the note, and why—now more than ever—I *really* wanted to meet the student.

"If you could tell her that you and I have met, and if I bring her your note . . ." I shut up, hoping that I hadn't sounded as manipulative to Gene as I had to myself.

He sighed deeply and gestured for me to follow him. We walked through a sliding door and out onto a balcony overlooking the restaurant next door. He leaned over the ledge. I followed suit and waited for him to speak.

Finally, he turned to face me. "I'm protective of Cat. She's a big girl and can take care of herself, lord knows. But everybody wants a piece of her. Bottom line, it's not my place—or desire—to meddle in her affairs."

"Fair enough," I said, trying not to look as disappointed as I felt.

He gave me a conciliatory pat on the back and, after a long pause, told me that he'd spoken with Charles just before I'd called.

"Now he's someone who's *very* protective of Cat. In a sense, that's part of his job. I promised him that I wouldn't reveal her identity to you—and I've already blown it."

"I guess you could say the Cat's out of the bag!" I laughed, taking too much pleasure in my own pun.

"Yeah. Funny."

"Charles told you about my 'schooling' in GTY?"

"Of course."

"From what I can gather, you've been instrumental in the development of the principle."

"Oh, I don't know that I'd go that far. I've just always done what's come naturally to me. As a guitar teacher, anyway."

"I'd love to hear your take on it, if you don't mind."

"Hoping you'll earn an audience with Cat, are you?"

"Well, sure. But I have to say that I'm really intrigued by what I've learned about Greater Than Yourself from Charles and from Plumeria Maple. My instincts tell me that there's something deeply significant about GTY."

"I think your instincts are on the money. GTY is simple on the surface, but it's nothing less than revolutionary in the workplace. I say that as a businessman, not as a guitar teacher."

"Would you mind telling me about how you came to develop the Greater Than Yourself philosophy?"

"Not at all," he said, gazing out across the balcony's railing. "First, I never called it by that name, or by GTY—or by any name. It's just the way I taught. I'm not sure who was the first to label it—maybe Cat, maybe one of her business mentors.

"As a teacher I always thought of Greater Than Yourself this way: It's not my job just to raise the skill level of my students; my job is to do whatever I can to make sure that when we're done working together—or, eventually, as a result of our having worked together—my student will be a *better* guitarist than I am. Sometimes it happens, sometimes not. Some students understand what they're being offered and dive in with full commitment; others want to learn just enough to get the girls."

"I can understand that," I said, thinking back to high school, and my first guitar. It had brought about significantly improved results in my courtship abilities, if you know what I mean.

I reflected back for a moment on the few great school, university, and music teachers I'd known over the years—would they have described their roles the same way Gene had?

"Parents understand this concept instinctively," he continued. "Do you have kids?"

"Yep. Three. Grown and gone and doing well."

"As well as you?"

"Better than I was at their ages, I think."

"How do you feel when they're having a hard time with something?"

I felt the answer to Gene's question before I could put it into words. "Like someone's yanking my heart out of my chest with a hot pair of pliers," I said.

"And when your kids succeed at something they worked hard at, or experience some kind of a triumph?"

"The greatest feeling in the world. Euphoric."

"Would you say you're happier about their successes than you are about your own?"

"Yes," I said without hesitation. "Yes, I am. No question."

"So," he went on, "you want them to have lives that are happier, more fulfilling, meaningful, productive, successful than your own. Is that right?"

"Yes," I said. "Although I want those things in my life, too."

"Yes, of course you do. And you also understand that the greatness in their lives doesn't in any way diminish yours, right?"

"Of course," I echoed.

"It's a parent's instinct—good, psychologically healthy parents, anyway. We want to elevate our children, boost them up above ourselves. We want to give them every opportunity to succeed. We give ourselves over to them completely—oftentimes at great personal risk and sacrifice. At our own peril. Well, in my estimation, great teachers have the same instincts, with the same hopes and dreams, for their students."

I hadn't thought about teaching or parenting in precisely this way before, but I was right there with Gene on all of it.

"But for some reason," Gene went on, sounding a little wistful, "we tend to check that great, wonderful, giving instinct at the door when we go to work. We assume that the rules of the game are different there."

I thought about that. "Well, they are, aren't they?"

"No. They are not," he said, insistent. "We just think they are."

"But," I argued, "the circumstances are completely different. Your kids aren't competing with you. There's no battle for title or position. I'll always be Dad, and they'll be my son or daughter, whatever else happens. At work, we're all competing with each other to get ahead, and there are only so many top positions to go around, right?"

"True enough," said Gene.

"And your students aren't vying for your place, either. At work, though, you're competing for the same resources and positions."

Surprisingly, the more I talked, the more vehemently I found myself in the devil's advocate's corner, and I wasn't used to that corner in this kind of discussion. I was the guy always coming down in favor of human-kindness-at-work. I'd written two books about the role of love in business, and I deeply believed every word I'd ever written on the subject. But what I said to Gene was also true. It's one thing to help others in the way that parents and teachers do, and quite another to help colleagues at work and make yourself obsolete in the process.

"On the surface, you're right, Steve. And the vast majority of businesspeople would agree with you. And there was a time when I would have agreed with you, too."

"But not anymore?"

"No, not anymore. I've come to see that limited opportunity—at work or anywhere else—is more illusion than reality. An illusion that we perpetuate by believing that success is a zero-sum game.

"Simply put, my helping you succeed doesn't require that I fail or falter. And my helping to launch you ahead of myself does not put me farther behind. Boosting you over my head doesn't lower me one inch."

"But it doesn't raise you up, either," I said. I paused to carefully consider my next words.

"Listen, Gene. I think that altruism is a noble quality in a person, I really do. But if all I'm doing at work is giving everyone else a boost, where, at the end of the day, does that leave me? It seems to me like I'd be ending up alone at the bottom of a well, staring up at everyone's butts as they scamper over the top and disappear into the light."

"That's because you're standing in the wrong metaphor, Steve. You're not standing in a well at all."

"Okay," I said, playing along. "Give me a better one."

"You're standing in an elevator."

"So, as I'm boosting people over my head . . ."

"You have to ensure that your floor is rising, too."

I knew I could argue the finer points of the metaphor, but I recognized that Gene was referring to Plumeria's principle of expanding yourself. So I took another tack.

"So, you practiced the idea of Greater Than Yourself in your insurance career?" I challenged, letting on that I'd done some homework on him before showing up.

A shadow seemed to fall over his face, and he looked down at the cement floor.

"I'd like to be able to claim that it was the secret to my success, that I was this shining example of everything we're talking about. But, regrettably, I can't. Truth is, I didn't really get it until the end of my career. If I'd been one iota as effective a leader as I was a guitar teacher . . ." He left the thought hanging in the air.

"So, practicing GTY at work is *theory*, as far as you're concerned," I tried to say gently. "It's not something you ever actually did."

"I did once," he said, his face flushing.

"What happened?" I asked.

"It was a disaster."

Gene Zander had been a master of his avocation of playing and teaching the guitar, but he was also quite adept at his vocation of insurance executive, a lifestyle that he chose over the prospects of the life of an itinerant, starving bluesman. Early in his career as a field salesman, he told me, he had quickly become the top producer in his region by practicing the very basics of Relationship Selling 101: Know your customers, listen to their problems, and do whatever it takes to make and keep them happy. It always amazed him that the struggling salespeople in the ranks never got what he considered to be a very simple principle: Put your desire for commissions last, and you'll make more money than anybody. To Gene it wasn't a paradox at all—it was just good business. And it felt right, too.

That was nearly forty years ago, he explained, at a time when "relationship" was hardly even a part of the business vocabulary. He was just going on his instinctive knowledge of what made people tick, a way of thinking that he took with him from the field into the corporate offices when he got his first major promotion.

Gene Zander had been golden; back then he could do no wrong. The rapidly expanding pieces of the company under his command consistently produced near the top of the industry. Everybody wanted to work for him; he was, by his own account, a very happy—and increasingly wealthy—young man.

"And this had nothing to do with making your employees greater than yourself?" I interjected.

"No, it didn't. Don't get me wrong; I wasn't a jerk. I was respectful of others, and a great listener, and I tried to inspire others to work hard by working harder than anybody. But the thought of raising anyone in my business above myself, as I tried to do with my guitar students? It never even occurred to me.

"That is, until I met and hired Sarah. She was a new B-school graduate—a place I'd never been myself—and the most gifted strategic thinker I'd ever seen. She had more natural, uncultivated talent in one eyelash than I had in my whole body. I knew—*knew*—that if I gave her the right kind of guidance and opportunity she could eventually run the whole company. And Steve, the thought that one day I could end up reporting to her? Not only did that not threaten me, it inspired me."

"So, what happened?"

"She had one major disadvantage. A disadvantage that— I swear—never dawned on me until it was too late."

"What was the problem?" I urged.

"She was a woman."

I looked at him, agape.

"It was like I abruptly woke up to discover that even though I was still fairly young, I was considered one of the good ol' boys—the club that ran the company. I never saw an actual sign that said NO GIRLS ALLOWED, but there may as well have been."

"What woke you up?"

"The minute that I put Sarah up for a promotion for vice president, I stopped getting invited to play golf. People started avoiding me in the hallways. Happy hour at the local hangout wasn't so happy anymore."

"They shunned you?" I said, amazed.

"I'm sure there are still places like that today, but it was far more commonplace back then. I didn't understand it."

"So what did you do?"

He shifted his weight uncomfortably. "I withdrew Sarah's nomination."

"You didn't." I regretted it as soon as I said it—Gene was obviously deeply disappointed in himself to this day over his actions; he didn't need for me to rub salt in the wound.

"Yes, I did. Sarah quit; I worked harder than ever, and in two blinks of an eye the years were gone and I was facing sixty. I'd risen to the level of senior executive vice president and was the heir-apparent to the CEO position. A lot of people thought I'd lost my mind when I decided to retire early and teach guitar."

"So your passionate discourse about GTY at work . . ."

"Is not from my direct experience, no," he said. "I was a good executive. Some say I was a legend in the industry, to a degree. And I'm not complaining about the money I made. But I do wonder how much more I could have done for myself, for others, and for the company, if I'd taken a stand on my principles—starting with Sarah—and really boosted at least a few people over my head along the way. What I always try to do in my role as teacher."

We walked back inside, I picked up my guitar case, and we headed down the hall toward the door.

"I don't mean to be difficult about this, Gene. But I still don't understand why you're so convinced that Greater Than Yourself is a viable thing at work. As a former executive, you're *philosophically* convinced about it, I can see. But practically speaking, by your own admission, you have never actually seen it work that way."

"I'm convinced because I've watched someone else do it."

"Cat?" I said.

"Yes. And others." He gave me a welcome, mischievous smile. "Perhaps you should talk to her about it yourself."

"Ya *think*?" I laughed. "Care to hook a fella up? Seriously, Gene. I really need to meet Cat. I mean, don't you think this guitar is some kind of a . . . I don't know . . . sign?"

"You should take very good care of it—it's a fine instrument," he said, sidestepping my question. "Keep this note, too; it may be worth something someday." I took the old sheet of paper from him as he opened the door.

"And I wish you the best of luck with your journey into Greater Than Yourself, Steve. Charles told me about the vow you took to practice the philosophy. I wish someone had held me to that standard a long time ago. I'm confident you'll find it a rich experience in many ways."

As I walked out to my car, a noise from above caused me to look up at the balcony where Gene and I had been standing. I saw Cal peering down at me, his face just barely clearing the banister.

"Hey, Bosco!" he stage-whispered. "Are you being fol-lowed?"

I looked up and down the street, playing along.

"Doesn't seem so."

A shadow of disappointment passed over his face. Then he pointed down at me like a preacher from the pulpit. "Don't feed the mullet!" he shouted.

And he was gone.

When I got home, the pressure in my head felt like a pent-up fire hose. I bent over my bathroom sink, turned on the faucet, and cupped some cool water in my hands.

It's not that GTY was a particularly difficult concept to grasp. The practice of making others greater than yourself might not be easy—particularly in the context of today's dog-eat-dog business world—but it wasn't like my brain hurt from trying to process complex data or some such thing. It hurt from something less familiar.

I thought back through the day's rapid-fire events, meetings, and conversations and searched for the source of my disturbance. Expand yourself? Made perfect sense. Give yourself? Yeah, sure. Of course. The promise of the Golden Rule. Replicate yourself? Pay it forward. Can't argue with that. I even saw the movie.

So, what was it?

I splashed the water over my face and looked up into the mirror, watching the beads roll down and over my lips. And then I remembered the vow I had taken.

I'd sworn to practice first; preach later. No wonder I had a headache. It wasn't the concept of GTY I was struggling with; it was the reality.

"Hey, Bosco," I said to myself in the mirror. "No kidding now. Are you capable of doing this?" I jabbed at my reflected forehead, leaving print smudges on the glass.

"Can you name one person—just one—that you can honestly say you're trying to elevate above yourself?"

I groped for a towel, patted my face dry, and walked out into the living room. Through the window I could see the lights reflecting on the evening water of Mission Bay as I picked up the Gibson and settled onto the couch. I strummed absently, trying to remember the events in my life that had brought me here.

I didn't go to journalism school or join the debate club to get to where I was professionally. I was an entrepreneur who came up through the school of Taking It Repeatedly on the Chin.

In the beginning, I wanted to be a musician. I wanted to sing and write and play the guitar and travel around the country, to be creative and inspiring and whatnot. It was a fine dream, too. The only problem was that it smacked right up against my other dream of having a family and raising kids and helping them to grow up and be smart and kind and *fed* and whatnot.

I got married at twenty-three and we started having children right away. And before I knew it, my two dreams had collided like North- and South-going Zaxes. It didn't take a Dr. Seuss to tell me that one of them had to give. So I got myself a job in the financial services industry, one that I would eventually parlay into a company of my own.

Abandoning the music path was so painful for me that I put my guitar in a closet and couldn't even look at it for years. In order to become a responsible, money-earning adult and dad, I'd cut off and stuffed away a big, important part of myself. I never had any doubt that I'd pursued the right path; shunning the music was just my way of coping with the sacrifice associated with that choice.

As the years clipped by I increasingly reembraced the guitar and came to appreciate its place in my life as a comfort, an outlet, a way to stay in touch with my idealistic, youthful zeal, my uninhibited expressiveness. Playing gave me space to think, to reflect, to—dare I say it—*be*.

So now here I was: sitting on my couch, having just clicked past the half-century mark in the age department, strumming and picking just like I had when I was a teenager. Except that now I wasn't thinking about my future; I was taking inventory of my past, of my GTY track record.

Even though their mother and I had eventually divorced, my kids had turned out well. They were grown and gone and—I'll admit to some bias here—were terrific young adults. Could I have done better when they were little? Of course. Could I do better for them now that we're all grown up? I admit that I hadn't thought about that before today—at least not in the specific context of making them greater than myself. The prospect of a reinvigorated relationship with my kids sent a quiet thrill through my body.

What about professionally, though? Whom could I point to that I'd really, significantly boosted up over myself? When had I freely and fully given of myself, and had I ever really given others the full repertoire of my knowledge, my contacts, my resources, and my time?

No, not really.

It's uncanny how fast a thrill can turn chill.

To give myself a little credit, I found it fairly easy to name at least a few former colleagues of mine whom I'd helped—aspiring speakers, for example, whom I'd hooked up with some very influential players in the industry. I'd encouraged and advised them on their strategy and approach, their message and marketing, and I'd shared freely the lessons I'd learned from my own plentiful mistakes. And I'd done it because I'd wanted to, because it was the right thing to do for friends, and because it felt good to help.

Most were grateful; some were not. But did that matter?

Honestly, it did. I wanted them to appreciate my efforts on their behalf, my investment in their careers, and I'm not ashamed to say so.

I like to think of myself as a generous guy. But I wouldn't say I'm altruistic, because I wanted something in return—not money, not position, but thanks and appreciation.

All in all, I told myself, I was a good guy by most people's standards. When friends ask for help, I help, and before today I'd have gone to my grave patting myself on the back for being a generous, kindhearted human being.

That is, until this principle of Greater Than Yourself came along and completely changed the game. Calling myself merely "helpful" suddenly felt more like admonishment than praise.

I set the guitar flat in my lap and considered the vow I'd made earlier in the day. *Vow* is not a word to be used lightly. No preaching without the practice; no saying without doing. Remembering Plumeria's challenge, I was clear that I'd have to find someone in my life—my professional life, more specifically—who could become my own GTY project.

I would have to choose the right person and do so wisely.

To be blunt, I was not about to waste my time and squander my hard-earned contacts and credibility on someone who wouldn't rise wholeheartedly to the opportunities I had to offer, and the significant personal challenge it would mean for him or her.

Choose wisely, I told myself.

So, whom did I know that had the talent, desire, heart, and work ethic to leverage and use whatever it was I had to give?

The answer was suddenly as obvious as a stiff slap on a cold day.

When I first met Tommy Spaulding he was the thirty-six-year-old CEO of two nonprofit youth leadership organizations. One, Leader's Challenge, which he'd founded and started from scratch, had become Colorado's preeminent leadership program for high school students; the other, Up with People, was a world-renowned, forty-year-old cross-cultural program devoted to building bridges across the all-too-frequent international, cultural, and socioeconomic chasms that separate us human beings from one another.

Running either one of those endeavors would be an enormous undertaking—but two? At the same time? Unimaginable; yet, he was doing it—at least for the time being.

Having heard about me from a mutual friend, Tommy had been interested in having me speak at a fund-raising event for Leader's Challenge. Before he extended the invitation, however, he wanted to see me in action to make sure I could deliver the goods, so he had flown out to Las Vegas to watch me speak at another company's conference.

You know how it is when you lose touch with a dear, life-long friend and then, after many years, you reconnect like no time has passed? The fact that you've lived completely different lives and experienced vastly different things in the interim makes not one iota of a speck of a difference. Your love and affection for each other are as deep and strong as they were when you were kids, or in college, or in Scouts, all those ages and eons ago.

Well, it was like that when Tommy and I met that day in Las Vegas, except for the fact that we'd never met before.

Instant old friends.

I can't speak for what he saw in me, but I was immediately struck by Tommy's energy. Or, more accurately, I was struck by the fact that Tommy *was* energy. He bounded up to me after my speech, shook my hand with both of his, and so earnestly invited me to lunch with his wife, Jill, and beautiful baby girl, Caroline, that there was literally no way I could have declined.

Over lunch, Tommy told me about himself. How, at seventeen, after barely eking through high school (graduating, he's fond of saying, Thank God Almighty Cum Laude), he traveled the world with Up with People—an experience that opened his eyes and his heart. Over the years, he told me, he'd lived on four continents, traveled to over sixty countries, and stayed with hundreds of host families all over the world.

Because of his dyslexia, he had to study extra hard and long in college—he did not want to do an academic repeat of high school—and had to pay his own way through. So, on top of spending interminable hours in the library, he sold T-shirts, took odd jobs, launched several small entrepreneurial ventures, and finished his degree with a surplus of thirty-five thousand dollars in his checking account.

After graduating with a degree in political science, he

went on to work for the Olympics in Japan, get his MBA in Australia, and, after a brief stint as a superstar salesman for IBM, pursue his dream of giving back to the world by establishing Leader's Challenge.

He started the program in Denver, a town where, at first, he knew virtually no one in the business or political community—communities he'd have to rely on for funding and support. He sought out the most influential, successful businesspeople in town and went from office to office, zapping them with his vision, conviction, and—you can be sure of this—energy, until they finally began to figure out that this kid was just not going to go away.

Over time, he raised over five million dollars for Leader's Challenge and spread the program from Denver through the entire state of Colorado. And then one day, the Up with People board of directors came knocking and asked Tommy to take over the reins and shepherd that organization through a restructuring and relaunch. He loved Up with People for how it had changed his life, and Leader's Challenge was his baby that still needed his attention, so he did what no truly sane person would ever have done: He agreed to be the CEO of Up with People as long as he could continue being CEO of Leader's Challenge, too. And they did what no sane board would ever have done.

They said yes.

Needless to say, by the end of lunch I was having trouble catching my breath.

That was the start of a relationship that has continued to grow deeper, with Tommy's and my life becoming increasingly intertwined. Not only did he sign me up to speak at the fund-raiser, a little later he nominated me to join Up with People's board of directors, an invitation that I gladly accepted. And as we spent more time together, we began to learn—as good friends inevitably do—about each other's hopes, dreams, and aspirations.

Tommy gave the introductory remarks at that fund-raiser in Denver, and his talent and electricity as a speaker were immediately and abundantly clear. What I've come to know since, though, is that he wants to expand on that talent and establish a presence on the so-called speakers' circuit. In short, Tommy wanted to do what I do.

And there, I now saw, was my Greater Than Yourself sweet spot.

And right then and there I made a second vow, a vow that could literally change both our lives in an intensely personal way: I would—after getting Tommy's full agreement with and commitment to the task at hand—do everything I could, share all that I had learned, give all my connections and contacts so that, in time, Tommy Spaulding would be a significantly better, more famous, more influential public speaker, figure, and thought leader than I.

I had no doubt that he'd be up for that, although, given his humility, I knew he'd be more than a little uncomfortable with the idea of "surpassing" me.

He'll get used to it, I thought.

Given that I'd just sworn myself to a major undertaking—and hopefully not the kind of undertaking that ends up with my being planted six feet under—I knew I needed to do something to hold myself ridiculously accountable, as Charles would say, to my own pledge. It's not that I didn't feel fully committed to Project Spaulding, but I really wanted to be sure that nothing fell through the cracks, what with my crazy travel schedule and all.

There are few things I claim to know with absolute certainty, but one of them is this: Nothing on this fine Earth turns up the accountability heat like the blazing eyes of public scrutiny.

Now I knew what to do with Plumeria's gift of the domain name.

I would use www.GreaterThanYourself.com as a public—very public—place to document my Greater Than Yourself experience with the life and career of Tommy Spaulding. I would show, in real time, what I was doing, how Tommy was responding, and what successes happened as a result.

That also meant, of course, that the world would see what *didn't* work. There was, in other words, the very likely possibility that the whole Web community would—with a ripe mixture of consternation and glee—would watch me flail and fall like a donkey on skates. I felt a cold sweat break out on my palms.

I parked my guitar for the night. Then, clearing a space on the dining room table, I set down my laptop, fired it up, opened the browser, and went to the setup page for my Web site. After a long, deep breath, I typed up a few words and launched myself headlong into the blogosphere.

GTY Project Spaulding was open for business.

> > > > > > > **CHAPTER** 17

Not long ago, hearing a certain cheery electronic voice in my computer would have rocketed ripples of anticipation up my spine. And I wasn't the only one. That friendly little voice became a cultural icon to millions of Internet neophytes. It embodied the warmth of acknowledgment and connection in an increasingly cold and isolated technological world. In effect, it said to us, "You are not a loser! Someone cares!" Literally, it said to us, "You've got mail!"

Call it divine providence or natural selection, but over time a dull vibration in my cell phone had usurped the digital Smurf in my laptop. But the excitement was still there because it meant not that someone had e-mailed me, but—even better—that I'd been *texted*.

That was how, after staying up till the wee hours working on my new blog, my day had started on that fine Friday morning. My cell gave one quick, dull buzz and the screen lit up with a line that would have made no sense, would have never even been written, back in the Neanderthal days of my youth:

U up yt?

I cracked my knuckles, shook out my thumbs, and engaged Charles in a prime example of modern, electronic discourse.

Yep

Meet me?

4?

Choosing not to answer my question, he texted instead an address in the suburbs and a time of the morning that gave me just enough margin to shower and shave. Making a quick decision to comply, I summoned up my best, most efficient rejoinder.

K, I thumbed.

Soon I was driving away from Mission Beach and heading toward the burbs of North County, San Diego. The road gnomes at MapQuest had instructed me to exit the 15 freeway and drive inland several miles to a major intersection in a town called Poway, which billed itself as "The City in the Country" but looked like neither.

I turned into the parking lot of a strip mall that had seen better years but was showing the early signs of a renovation. At the far end of the lot, work crews were perched on scaffolding, administering to the property some kind of a structural face-lift, a project that, so far, had only served to remove the addresses of the individual units.

Given that I had no other information about our meeting place, I figured I'd just park the car and wander around until I could raise Charles on the cell and get personally guided in for a landing.

As it turned out, that wouldn't be necessary.

The blue neon sign in the window said HAIR SALON, but that's not what gave the place away; rather, it was the name of the establishment that clanged the startling bell of recognition in my head.

The sign over the door presented the bizarre set of words that I'd heard for the first time just the day before. At Gene Zander's studio. From the mouth of Cal, his quirky, electric Kool-Aid brother.

Shaking my head in astonishment, I crossed the parking lot, walked up to the plate-glass window, and tried to peer inside to see whether Charles was there. The glare from the sun hurt my eyes, so I took a step back and looked again at the sign over the door.

No doubt about it. This had to be the place; the coincidence would have been too great. The sign's hand-painted words all but demanded that I open the door and walk in.

DON'T FEED THE MULLET, it read.

I stepped up to the reception desk and looked around as my eyes slowly recovered from the window's reflected sunlight. At first glance, the place had all the obvious trappings of a hairstyling establishment. There were six barber chairs, three on each side of the large, mirrored room, each with its own armoire filled with the supplies and artillery necessary for a constant series of assaults on both male and female heads. A curtained area toward the back housed a row of shampooing stations of sinks and reclining chairs. I don't know what a hairstylist's chemicals are called, but I know what they smell like, and this place's olfactory environment was typical of any other's.

I think my brain noticed all those things first in order to give me something normal and familiar to latch on to because, other than the elements common to any similar business, this place was anything but ordinary.

Where most salons' walls were adorned with fashion photos of sunken-cheeked, perfectly coiffed models, this place had giant, full-color posters of Stevie Ray Vaughan, Jimi Hendrix, Janis Joplin, and Big Mama Thornton pictured in various iconic poses that make up the stuff of blues and rock legend. And while the wall decor was unusual, the furnishings were off the charts.

The middle space between the styling chairs served as the waiting area, which housed the usual magazine racks, armchairs, and small tables—and even those old standards leaned decidedly to the funky side, style-wise—but it was all the other stuff that made this place a challenge to categorize in any conventional way.

Pushed up against the back wall was a full drum kit—bass, snare, tom-toms, cymbals, cowbells, all of it—flanked on either side by a modest but adequate stack of amplifiers. A few empty guitar and microphone stands stood strategically positioned in front of the layout, completing the look and feel of a band's practice space. Off to the side, an old, beat-up acoustic guitar of undetermined origin leaned casually against a comfortable-looking, armless, quilt-covered chair.

I was so immediately taken by all the equipment in the place that it took me a moment to register the fact that there were quite a few people in there, too.

In fact, the chairs were filled with male and female customers whose hair was in various stages of pruning, shaping, drying, or dyeing by a collection of raucous and jovial stylists who seemed to emit an endless barrage of shouting, singing, and laughing.

Charles Roland occupied the first chair on the left. Towering behind him, scissors in hand, was a tall, wide, muscular Pacific Islander with a smooth, shaved head that gleamed as bright as the broad smile on his face.

They were both looking at me and laughing, obviously entertained by the perplexed look on my face as I surveyed the scene. They'd been watching me since I walked in, and now the big, bald, scissor man was gesturing for me to join them.

He shifted the scissors to his left hand and grasped my

hand with his right as I positioned myself next to where Charles was sitting.

"What's crackin', brah!" the stylist said warmly, a slight trace of the islands in his voice. "Welcome to the Mullet. I'm Jeffery Kepeli—the owner."

I returned his smile.

"What do you think we call him, Farber?" Charles flicked my arm with the back of his hand. "Go on. Take a guess."

This could be a dangerous game with someone that large holding a pair of very sharp scissors.

"I'm a lousy guesser," I said, opting out.

"Ahhh, c'mon, brah. What are you afraid of? Offending me? No worries; thick skin." He smacked himself on his massive bicep, a gesture that wasn't as comforting as he probably intended it to be.

"Ummm," I said, stalling. "Tiny?"

They looked at each other and laughed.

"Try again," said Charles.

"Mr. Clean? Gigantor?" They laughed again.

Another stylist, a younger guy with a vine tattoo running up his left cheek, took pity on me.

"Hey, Big Jeff! Give the dude a break," he shouted. "Just tell him, already."

"Wait," I said. "I've got it. Is it Big Jeff?"

"Yeah, it is." He scowled and then brightened. "But I like Gigantor, brah. That's got possibilities!" Holding the clippers, he tilted Charles's head with his fingertips. "Or Godzilla. I like that, too."

"Ahhh! You can't pick your own nickname, Big Jeff," called out the vine-faced stylist. "You are, and will always be, Big Jeff. It's a universal law, mate!"

"So, Big Jeff," I said to him while my eyes panned the room's music equipment again. "What goes on here?"

"What goes on here, brah, is just a little of what they call work-life balance. This is the day job," he said as he clipped a shock of Charles's already short hair for emphasis. "And that"—he gestured to the setup—"is my passion."

"Big Jeff is an amazing bass player," said Charles. "Don't Feed the Mullet is both his business and his rehearsal space."

"One beast feeds the other," said Big Jeff as he stepped back and surveyed the progress on Charles's head.

"But not the mullet," I offered.

"Never! Don't feed the mullet! The mullet must die and never return!" he shouted, raising his scissors high in the air.

And suddenly, every stylist in the place and more than a couple of customers stopped their conversations midsentence and shouted in perfect unison, "The mullet must die!"

"Meaning the hairstyle and not the fish, I take it," I said, taken aback by the hilarious, obviously traditional outburst.

"Big Jeff is nothing if not a man of strong opinions on style and grooming," said Charles, brushing his own hair off the black-and-white checkered cloth draped over his body.

"That I am," Big Jeff concurred, a smirk on his lips. "And music. Pretty strong opinions on that, too."

"Tell Steve about tonight," Charles said.

"Tonight . . . big jam session here, brah. It'll be awesome. You should come by."

"And he should bring his guitar, right?"

"Oh yeah, no doubt. Bring your axe, brah. You are welcome to join in. Come ready to play. We'll have a pretty good audience, too."

Even though I'd swapped a few licks with Gene Zander

the day before, it had been a long time since I'd actually played in public, so Big Jeff's invitation filled me with a mix of pure excitement and abject terror. Playing alone on my couch I still had as much confidence as Clapton, but making my fingers work on a stage in front of a band of accomplished musicians and a gaggle of spectators was something else entirely.

"I don't know, Big Jeff. I don't want to hold you guys back. I don't get to play much."

"No worries, Steve. If you suck you can always just kill the volume and pretend to play rhythm."

That seemed like more of a dare than a solution.

"C'mon, Steve," said Charles. "You'll love it. You'll be really glad you came."

I agreed, of course, secretly elated beyond belief. Even though I was ridiculously rusty, nothing was more fun than a jam session.

"So, Charles," I said, getting to business. "Other than the great pleasure of meeting Big Jeff and the crew, is there any particular reason you asked me here?"

"Well, given what I heard about what Gene told you, I thought today would be a good day for you to meet Cat," he said, feigning nonchalance. "Would that work for you?"

I looked around the Mullet.

"No, she's not here. I'm going to take you over to the YSC offices in downtown San Diego. If you have the time, that is."

Yes! I thought.

"Yeah, I think that'd work." I looked at my watch as if I were taking a mental assessment of the pressing issues on my plate, calculating how I could fit a meeting with Cat Cassidy into my crazy schedule.

"When?"

"I thought we'd drive over there when Big Jeff is done with his artwork," said Charles, pointing up at his head.

"Pull a chair over here, brah." Big Jeff pointed to a few empty ones against the back wall near the drums. "He ain't leaving until I'm done with him, so you may as well kick back and relax."

I grabbed a folding chair from the other side of the room, carried it over to a space between Big Jeff's station and the window, and sat down with a sigh.

"You comfy?" asked Big Jeff.

I nodded, half-smiling. Truth is, I *was* comfy. I loved the feeling of this place, and Big Jeff's ease and charisma were contagious.

"Good. Because I'm gonna tell you a story, Mr. Farber"— he flickered his scissors for emphasis—"a story of a great, unassuming, and humble man."

Charles rolled his eyes as if to say, *Oh boy, here it comes.*

"Okay," I said. "Who's that?"

Big Jeff swung Charles's chair around clockwise so the two of us were sitting face-to-face.

"You're looking at him, my man . . . Charles 'Sucky Chucky' Roland."

Now this I had to hear.

I'd never actually seen Charles blush before and it looked kind of out of place on his face, like sunburn on a shut-in.

"Hey, look. Your ears are glowing, Chucky," said Big Jeff from his vantage point behind Charles's head. "What'd I say, brah? Humble."

"So, Charles," I said, feeling my curiosity stir. "What's your story, then?"

"He won't tell you." Big Jeff shook his head, smiling.

"Too humble?"

Big Jeff nodded. "So it falls to me to tell the story of little Chuck Roland and his sixth-grade epiphany."

I stretched my legs out in front of me and waited for Big Jeff to continue.

"Mostly, I was born and raised in Hawaii," he said. "But we moved here to San Diego for a few years. Middle school years, for me. Sixth, seventh, and eighth grade. Chuck was the first kid I met on my first day of school. I was really nervous. I felt totally out of place. New kid or not, I stuck out like a sore thumb anyway because of my size. I was Big Jeff even back then."

"You were Big Jeff on the day you were born, according

to your mama," interjected Charles. That earned him a quick, affectionate slap on the back of his head.

"My story, Chucky. You be quiet for once. Anyway, I sat in front of him in class and he immediately tapped me on the shoulder, introduced himself, and welcomed me to the school. I thought that was pretty cool at the time, but looking back I see how extraordinary that was. You know what I mean, brah?"

Of course I did. Schoolkids aren't exactly famous for their open acceptance of the new and unusual.

"We became instant friends. Hung out together at recess and after school, got to know each other's families. All of it. That kind of friend, you know?"

I did.

"Well, one day the principal of the school came into our class, which was always a big deal. Usually meant that someone was in trouble. Or there was a lice outbreak or something. But on that day, he was just paying us a visit. Wanted to chat, to connect with the huddled middle-school masses, I guess.

"Turns out, though, that the principal's surprise visit was the first day of the rest of Chucky's life."

"Indeed it was," said Charles, flicking a couple of strands of hair off his arm.

"So, the principal stands in front of the class and gives a little talk about how we may think we're just kids and all, but that the rest of our lives is bearing down on us like a freight train on a flock of sheep."

"He didn't say it like that," Charles protested.

"My story! Or would you rather take it from here?"

"Go on," said Charles. "Sorry."

"Anyway," Big Jeff continued, "he tells us we should start thinking about what we want to be when we grow up. *Does anyone already know?* he asks us. And, much to his surprise, almost every hand in the room shot up in the air.

"Delighted, the principal claps his hands and says, 'Well, let's go around the room. Everybody can tell the whole class what he or she wants to be.'

"So, the first kid says *fireman,* and the next says *President of the United States,* and another says *policeman,* and *actress,* and *doctor* and he's getting closer to me and I'm getting really nervous because I never speak up in class. And then he points to me—and he knows me because I was new and big and Hawaiian and all—and he says, 'Mr. Kepeli? What about you?'

"And I said the first thing that came to my mind. 'I want to be a totally kick-butt bass player in a rock-and-roll band,' I said. The principal scowled at my language and the class started hooting and hollering and I became an instant celebrity."

"Everybody loved him after that," said Charles.

"So the teacher calms everyone down and makes me apologize to the principal for saying 'butt,' which I did. And then it was Charles's turn.

"'What about you, son?' he says to Charles. 'What do you want to do?' And Charles thinks for a minute—which he almost always did before he said anything in class—and then says that what he really wanted was to help the other kids become what they wanted to be.

"And the class blew a gasket all over again—laughing and

shouting like they'd just heard the funniest thing ever. But this time they weren't cheering, they were jeering and mocking like this was the lamest, dumbest thing they'd ever heard anyone say. And over the teacher's efforts to calm the class down, one kid's voice rose as clear as a lunch bell.

" 'That's because you suck at everything, Chuck!' "

"And there it was. The word stuck to him like burrs on a poodle. Within hours he was known throughout the school as Sucky Chucky."

"A name that stayed with me all through high school, until I left for college and started with a clean slate," said Charles, with no hint of sadness or resentment. "Almost every day after that fateful classroom visit, someone would come to me and say something like, 'Hey, Sucky Chucky! Are you gonna help me today?' Or, 'How about you do my homework?' Or, simply, 'You suck, Chuck!' "

"That's terrible," I said, incredulous at how mean his classmates had been. "That's an awful story. Nothing personal, Charles," I said, looking at Big Jeff. "But in what possible, conceivable way is that story supposed to be inspiring? Are you saying Charles's humiliation as a child made him the man he is today?"

"No, brah, that's not what I'm saying at all. Let me finish. First of all, on that day in class, Charles became absolutely clear on what he wanted to do with his life. How many sixthgraders do you know of that can say that?"

"Not many," I said.

"And he meant it, brah. The very first thing he did after school that day was come to my house and persuade my parents—I wish I could remember exactly what he said, because it was awe-inspiring to my young ears—to buy me an electric bass and sign me up for lessons at the local music store. And they did it. And I practiced and played every day since. I ultimately decided that the musician's lifestyle wasn't for me, but I'll tell you this without bragging: I can play in any band—rock, blues, jazz, whatever—anywhere in the world. You know why?"

"Why?" I asked.

He grinned wide. "Because I'm a totally kick-butt bass player, brah. By anyone's standards. Thanks to Chucky here."

He patted Charles on the head.

"But what makes Charles Roland great—and this is the truly amazing thing—is that *eleven-year-old* Chucky committed the rest of his life to the task of making others great."

Soon I would discover how true that really was.

Charles and I rode together to the offices of YSC Corporation. Leaving his car at the Mullet was his idea. He'd assured me that he'd be getting a ride back there later that evening for the jam session (not a player himself, he was a devoted audience member), so we both hopped in my ride and motored back toward downtown San Diego.

On the way, Charles gave me a quick snapshot of YSC. Some of the story, of course, I already knew. A staffing company of sorts—they preferred to think of and describe themselves as a talent agency—they helped to place technology stars with some of the country's largest corporations. It was a privately held company with a culture that was, according to Charles, youthful, passionate, and energetic.

Low turnover, blazing growth (it was listed as one of the fastest-growing companies in the United States several years in a row), and record profits made YSC a company to watch, especially if they ever decided to go public.

Cat Cassidy was the second CEO, having taken the reins from the founder. And she was newsworthy, not only because she was young, smart, attractive, and full of spunk, but because she brought home stellar results for her clients and her company. She was also articulate and photogenic, which yielded her quite a few write-ups in the business press.

"You know why I had been looking at the guitar you bought at Vintage Brothers?" Charles asked me.

I shook my head as I exited the 163 toward downtown.

"Because Cat told me about Gene's gift, about how she'd had to sell it to get cash to pay for her classes, and all the regrets she carried because of it. She had introduced me to Gene some time before, so I asked him to describe the guitar for me, and every now and then I'd stop in the music store and look for that model, just in case. And the other day, there it was. But you bought it before I could get Gene in there to check it out."

I shot him a quick glance over my right shoulder.

"You were going to buy it for her?" I asked. "An expensive guitar?"

"We love her," said Charles.

I felt a little guilty about getting to the Gibson first. But just a little. My anticipation at meeting Cat, however, was building. If Charles's feelings were any indication, Cat clearly engendered deep devotion among her staff. Something about her and the GTY philosophy had created a kind of fierce loyalty and love that I always looked for and rarely found in business.

We used Charles's parking pass to enter the building's garage and rode the elevator to the eleventh floor.

YSC's lobby was understated but tasteful. The receptionist greeted us with a cheery voice and a big smile, which gave me a very strong first impression of the company. Had her greeting been so warm because Charles was with me?

We walked through a door and entered an open area full of cubicles and conference rooms. After Charles's description of the place, I'd expected YSC to be abuzz with youthful energy and enthusiasm, and I wasn't disappointed. A cacophony of laughter and conversation filled the air, and as we stepped into the room, I was almost run over by a young man dashing down the hall. He shouted an apology over his shoulder as he raced by. One of the conference rooms housed some kind of a meeting. But instead of sitting around the table, the team stood, huddled in a corner like they were getting ready to run back on the field.

"Fridays are pretty quiet around here," said Charles, laughing, reading the delighted expression on my face.

"This is *quiet*?" I exclaimed.

"Yes, believe it or not. We have a policy that allows people to leave early on Friday if they need to get a jump on the weekend traffic. So, we're a little light this afternoon. C'mon," said Charles. "Cat's office is this way."

I followed him down the hall and around the corner. We stopped in front of a glass door that looked into a medium-sized corner office with a lovely view of the Coronado Bridge. I loved the look and feel of the furniture and the beauty of the setting. There was only one distressing element.

It was empty.

"Hmm," said Charles, thoughtfully rubbing his chin. "Looks like we missed her."

Most of us carry a silent editor in our head. When he's doing his job, he's the guy who strikes inappropriate or unwise words while they're still half-formed and unspoken, before they launch inexorably out of our mouths and lodge forever in the minds of those around us.

Well, my silent editor, it seemed, had also gotten an early jump on the weekend.

"What?" I growled at Charles. "Are you freaking kidding me? Didn't you tell her we were coming?"

Charles was remarkably understanding of my outburst. He shook his head and looked at the floor. "I'm really sorry. Give me a minute and let me see if I can track her down. Have a seat, Steve. I'll be right back."

"*You're* sorry," I mumbled. I walked over to an empty cubicle nearby and sat down heavily in a chair as a wave of guilt washed over me. I really shouldn't have unloaded on him like that. I leaned back in the chair, looked up at the ceiling, and let out a protracted puff of air.

"Ooooh," said a voice from the next cubicle over. "Stood up by the big boss lady."

I peered over into the neighboring cube to locate the source of that irritating, scoffing voice.

"Excuse me," I said, staring down at the top of a curly redhead. "Are you talking to me?"

The red-haired young man scooted his chair away from his desk and, pushing at the floor with his feet like he was steering a pedal boat, navigated out of his cube and into mine.

"Timothy." He stretched his hand out to me as he pulled up alongside. There was a slight blush on his youthful, fair-skinned face. He wore a light blue, button-down oxford shirt and a conservative blue-and-red tie with the knot loosened and slightly askew around his thin neck.

"I didn't mean for you to hear that." The blush on his face intensified as he looked around to be sure we were alone. "Cat doesn't usually blow people off. But"—he glanced around again and lowered his voice to a near whisper—"she ain't perfect, either, whatever they say."

"Why are you telling me this?" I said, annoyed at Timothy insinuating himself into the situation.

He threw his hands in the air. "Hey," he said, "never mind. Just trying to give you a little perspective, that's all. I've been here for a while and I know how this place operates. Just trying to do you a solid."

He began backing his chair up, but I stopped him and apologized. I had a strong sense that his wanting to talk had a lot more to do with his own state of mind than mine.

"I've been here for two years, man," he said, "and I'm still just doing glorified clerical work. But I work my tail off. Like, I could have left early today, but I didn't. And I sit right outside of Cat's office, so I know she sees what I do."

He spoke in anger, but he sounded more defeated than

mad, more hurt than resentful. As if he'd been an unfortunate casualty of capricious circumstances rather than the victim of a corporate conspiracy.

"You don't feel appreciated," I said, stating the obvious.

"Ahhh," he waved his hand at me. "It's not that so much."

I waited.

"It's more like being left behind. Seems like everyone else gets promoted or assigned to cool projects, and I'm still here workin' my butt off processing invoices and typing and stuff like that. I was hired the same day as five other people my age and experience. We were all pretty much right out of school. One of them left to work for another company, and the rest of them stayed at YSC and are off traveling around to New York and London and doing cool stuff like that."

He sighed.

"Sorry, Timothy," I said, feeling the coaching impulse burbling up inside me. I've often thought that I may have a bad case of Facilitator Reflux Disease. "But—and I don't mean to pry here—why do you think that is? Why are they getting the opportunities and not you?"

"Because I'm not a kiss-up," he said bitterly, revealing the kind of attitude that would hold anyone back.

"And they are?"

He nodded emphatically. "It's so ingrained around here. It's a cultural thing," he said, seeming a little embarrassed. "They call it GTY."

My jaw dropped in surprise. "GTY?" I repeated.

"Yeah," said Timothy. "Greater Than Yourself. It's Cat's management philosophy."

"I'm familiar with it," I said, confused as to how it had

suddenly gotten such a negative spin. "But you don't sound happy with it."

"It's not fair," he said. "Every one of those people I mentioned? My peeps? They all got GTYed by someone else higher up in the company."

I always found it hilarious how companies spawned their own unique vernacular. "*GTY*ed, huh?" I laughed.

He returned my laugh with a small, sad smile.

"So, nobody's made you their GTY project, is that it?"

Timothy looked surprised that I had grasped his meaning so quickly, so I told him about my recent education in the Greater Than Yourself philosophy.

"Well, if you want my opinion . . ." he started to say.

"Seems like you've already shared that, Timothy," I said, dismissively.

"Look, I get the idea behind it, I really do," he persisted. "Today's leaders should look for tomorrow's potential leaders and then help them get there. That's one part of Cat's philosophy. And I think that's smart because it's going to be really healthy for the company in the long run."

"What's the other part?"

"It's not just about the managers. It's supposed to apply to *everybody,* at *every* level. If there's something I'm really, really good at, I'm supposed to look for opportunities to share my expertise with someone else—someone with a desire and a knack for it, maybe. I'm supposed to invest in that person and share whatever I know. So that maybe they end up being better at it than me."

"You have a problem with that idea?"

"Yeah." He paused, choosing his words. "For one thing,

what if I do that for somebody else, and nobody's interested in my help?"

"Has that happened to you? Have you offered to help someone and been turned down?"

"No. But why should I? No one's ever gone out of their way to help me get ahead around here."

"Let me see if I'm tracking here, Timothy. You won't GTY anyone else," I said, "unless someone GTYs you first. Is that about right?"

"Why should I?" he repeated, his tone getting increasingly defensive.

"Quid pro quo. Is that it?"

"Look," he said, "I need this job. As long as I keep my head down and march ahead, the paycheck will keep coming. That's what it's all about for me at this point. I'm barely hanging on around here as it is. Why should I help the competition?"

It was a remarkably honest admission for Timothy to make to a total stranger, which just underscored the severity of his situation. If I was reading between the lines correctly, Tim wasn't so much condemning GTY as a principle. Instead, he was offering up a distress signal from someone whose talents didn't match up with his job. I would bet anything that no one was willing to invest in Timothy because Timothy was unwilling or unable to invest himself in YSC. It seemed obvious that the poor guy was desperately out of place at this company, but he saw himself as having no other options. It had become a vicious cycle that someone was going to have to break or this kid's misery was just going to deepen.

Too many people hand out advice too easily, I often find,

and I was occasionally guilty of being one of them. I'd come to realize, though, that the quality of my advice was directly proportional to the degree to which I actually knew the other person. I'd known Timothy for about the time it would take to walk a New York City block, so I decided to just keep my yap shut on the subject of his life and career. Timothy had a different idea.

"So, what do you think I should do?" he said with disarming earnestness.

I felt a gush of the Facilitator Reflux coming on. "Listen, Timothy," I said. "You don't know me from beans, and vice versa. Take any advice I have with a huge grain of salt, you know?"

He nodded.

"You sure you want to hear it?"

He nodded again.

"First of all, it sounds to me like you don't really have a problem with Greater Than Yourself at all, philosophically. It sounds like you would, in fact, love to be a part of the process. But for some reason that's not happening for you.

"Greater Than Yourself, the way I understand it, is about putting your personal ego aside and sharing freely of yourself with another. Sometimes you're on the giving end of that equation, and sometimes you're receiving. Sometimes you're doing both. Either way, there's a profound interpersonal exchange taking place. Both parties have to be open and willing—not just willing, but committed—to making it work.

"I think there's a very simple reason you're not experiencing that here at YSC. You don't like the work because it doesn't utilize your talents and interests. You're not sharing

with others because you don't really feel like you have anything to share. And no one's knocking on your door, either,
for pretty much the same reason. Am I in the ballpark?"

"For the most part."

"Okay." I took that as a yes. "And I think there's a pretty
clear solution for you."

"You do?" He perked up. "What is it?"

"You should quit," I said.

His face fell.

"Find another place to work, Timothy. A company or job
you'll love. A place where you can use your talents. Life's too
short, dude."

"But I need the money," he said, softly. "I can't afford to
quit now."

"So, start looking. Work hard while you're here, and
when you find the right opportunity you'll know it clear as
day. That'll be the time to jump. And once you do, come back
to the GTY idea and try it in the new place. I bet it'll be a
whole different experience for you. You'll be a pioneer on
GTY in another company!"

He let out a long sigh through his thin, pink lips. "I
should'a stayed in my cube," he said, wistfully.

"Sorry, Timothy. You asked; I gave you my opinion. But
that's all it is. My opinion. It's your life, you know?"

"Yeah," he said. "I know."

"Then act like it," I said.

It's easy to be a hard-guy when it comes to someone else's pile of woes. My own was another story. Timothy left to work on a project, and I was still sitting like a wallflower waiting for Charles to return. Normally, being left to wait like that would have raised my blood pressure a few clicks, but I was preoccupied with my conversation with Timothy.

At first I'd been thrown by the bad blood he felt about YSC and Cat—the "big boss lady," as he'd referred to her. But I came to understand where he was coming from. It occurred to me that I might very well be the only person, other than Timothy himself, who knew how much he was struggling. If this were such a great culture, and Cat so phenomenal a CEO, how could they miss his discontent? Was this evidence of a chink in the cultural armor? I wondered how many other "Timothys" might be lurking unnoticed in the halls of YSC Corporation.

In any event, as the minutes ticked away, it seemed less and less likely I would have a chance to ask Cat about that, or anything else.

I walked back down the hall in the direction of the office lobby. Maybe the receptionist could page Charles for me, who had dematerialized as effectively as Cat had.

Charles intercepted me at the end of the hallway, his arms stretched wide in a mea culpa.

"Steve. I'm so sorry. Something came up with one of our biggest clients, and Cat had to dash to put out a fire. It was a situation that she had to handle personally; otherwise, I'm sure she would have sent someone else."

He sounded overly defensive of her, which made me wonder if he was being completely truthful. Cat's a professional, so I'd think she would have had someone try to reschedule my visit before I showed up at the office. Was she avoiding me on purpose? If so, why? I had no nefarious intentions and, as far as I knew, no communicable diseases.

"Why didn't she call you?" I asked, hurt by how casually she had flown the coop. "You're her gatekeeper, aren't you?" Charles was a perfectionist; he wasn't the type to let something like this slip.

"Again, I apologize, Steve," said Charles. "All I know is that it had to be something very important for Cat to rearrange her schedule at the last minute."

His contrition was so sincere that I couldn't help but smile and let him off the hook.

As Charles walked me back to my car, I told him about my conversation with Timothy. I didn't feel like I was betraying a confidence; rather, I was hoping to get the kid some help inside the company. Charles didn't seem at all surprised at what I told him.

"The only reason Timothy's still with YSC," said Charles as he punched the floor number inside the parking elevator, "is because he's smart and works very hard. In other words, he keeps up his end of the work-for-compensation bargain. But that's all. Which is fine, really, if merely working at a job makes you happy. And it does, for some people."

"But not Timothy," I said.

"No. He wants more. It's too bad he's not finding satisfaction at YSC because he's a good person and a dedicated employee, in spite of it all. He deserves to find a fulfilling career. We'd like nothing more than for him to find happiness here. But I don't think that's going to happen."

"Will you talk to him? Maybe give him a little coaching?" I said. Charles would be a terrific sounding board for Timothy.

"No, I won't."

I was stunned. "Why not?"

"Because he's covered. Timothy doesn't know it yet, but he's about to become someone's GTY project."

"That's awesome," I said, stunned again—in a good way this time. "Whose?"

The elevator stopped and the doors slid open. I stepped out into the parking lot and fumbled in my pocket for the car keys.

"Cat's," said Charles, as the door closed between us.

I woke up with a jolt. The room was dark and for a moment I didn't know where I was. I looked at the alarm clock and recognized it as my own.

Eight. I didn't even remember going to bed for the night, but more confusing was the complete absence of light in what is usually by this time of the morning a sun-filled room.

It made sense once I realized that it was 8:00 *p.m.*

Then I remembered. After my visit to YSC, when I returned home I decided to take a nap, so that I could be alert for tonight's jam session.

I bolted upright in bed and groped for the lamp switch. The jam session! They were starting right now. I obliterated the remaining cobwebs from my brain as I dashed to the shower, jumped in, washed, and dressed in record time. I grabbed the Gibson and a handful of picks and sprinted out to my car.

As I drove out to Poway, my panic gave way to the excitement of the prospect of a night of playing music. So I'd be late. No big deal. And even if they didn't want me coming up onstage in the middle of the session, I'd get to hear Big Jeff and his band. I wasn't 100 percent about performing anyway. Being a member of the audience would be just fine with me. I cranked up the volume on the car stereo and tapped the wheel as the music of Buddy Guy provided the soundtrack for the half-hour journey north.

The parking lot was jammed when I pulled into the strip mall. I parked at the far side near a mailbox and shipping store, which was dark for the night.

As I walked toward Don't Feed the Mullet, guitar case in hand, I found it odd that I couldn't hear even distant strains of music playing. These guys were electric, not acoustic. I'd have expected to at least feel the pulsing of a bass through the ether. But there was nothing. I had a fleeting sense of panic that I'd slept a full twenty-four hours and missed the whole thing—or gotten the date wrong. But that didn't explain why there were so many cars here.

The door to the shop was unlocked. I pushed it open and stepped into an empty space devoid of people. My heart sank when I saw that the drums and all the equipment were gone.

" 'Evening!" a voice behind me said, making me jump and nearly drop the guitar.

I spun around to see the vine-faced hairstylist sitting on a barber's chair, cloaked in the low light. "Sorry, mate. Didn't mean to scare you," he said.

"No worries," I said, sounding like I'd just sucked in a balloonful of helium. "Where is everybody?"

"It's all good," he said, jumping down from the chair. "I just stayed behind to catch the stragglers."

"Guilty," I said.

"We got word at the last minute that a lot of people were gonna show up, so we figured we better move to the bigger space in the back."

"The back?" I looked in the direction of the row of sinks.

"C'mon," he said. "I'll take you."

I followed him back past the sinks and down a dimly lit hallway whose entrance had been obscured by a curtain.

"Big Jeff and a partner converted the back of the building to a performance space and recording studio. It's nearly perfect, acoustically. Soundproof, too. That's why you don't hear anything—yet. It'll blow your mind when we walk in.

"They may turn it into a club someday, if they decide they want to invest the time and energy, but for right now, it's kind of like their personal playground. There's another entrance around the back, where the regulars know to go when we play for the public."

He turned the handle on a large, black metal door and pushed it open.

The sound came rolling at us like a wall of water, and I felt like I was entering a world-within-a-world. The place was packed, the stage flooded with color and white spotlights. A woman's bluesy voice blasted through the air like gravel wrapped in silk, singing a Robert Johnson classic:

I went down to the crossroads, fell down on my knees
Asked the Lord above for mercy, save me if you please.

Adjusting to the sudden sensory overload, I panned the room as best I could. I saw the heads of a sizable audience bobbing in unison; several people were dancing in the front. But I found it easier to focus on what was happening onstage.

Big Jeff was on the left corner of the stage, an electric bass slung around his massive neck. He wore a tank top, board shorts, and flip-flops, and spun and whirled as he thumped out a powerful bass line under the song.

Someone ripped into a screaming guitar solo, and I looked to the opposite side of the stage to see who was playing with such taste, feeling, and precision. Shredding on an old Fender Stratocaster, wearing an off-white linen sport jacket and black slacks, Gene Zander's white hair glistened under the illumination of the spotlight. He finished his solo, stepped back, and took a bow to acknowledge the thundering applause from the crowd.

Gene turned to face the middle of the stage and leaned into the nearest microphone.

"Take it, girl!" he yelled.

A young woman stepped forward, waiting until the beginning of the chord progression came around again to slide a thick, glass bottleneck up the neck of her guitar as the crowd screamed its approval.

The vine-faced stylist stepped up to the stage and yelled something into Gene's ear.

Gene cupped his right hand over his eyes to block the light as he looked out over the audience, until he caught sight of me standing in the back. "Come on up," he mouthed with a big smile on his face. He pantomimed playing on his guitar to indicate that I should bring mine.

My heart pounded as I made my way through the crowd and over to the side of the stage. Stage fright can make the simplest tasks nearly impossible to execute. My hands shook so hard that I was barely able to open the latches of the case and strap on my guitar. Somehow I managed to plug it in to a tuner and adjust the strings. I took a deep breath, stepped up next to Gene, and we exchanged a low five, jazz style. I plugged into the foot switch of an amp and turned to get a look at this woman who'd been kicking away on a killer slide solo.

Her jet black, bob-cut hair swayed as her head rocked from side to side. The small red stud in her nose matched the ruby gloss on her lips, and it all sparkled against the luminous backdrop of her smooth, white skin. She leaned her face toward the microphone and dropped her arms to her side as she sang.

I went down to the crossroads, tried to flag a ride.

She was wearing a short, tight-fitting, one-piece black knit dress that ended about midway down her thighs, which served to accentuate her legs.

I noticed she was barefoot; a piece of cartoon art was tattooed on the back of her left calf.

From the top of its tall, floppy, striped hat, to the mischievous grin, to the wide scarlet bow tie, it was a six-inch-tall, full-color tattoo of the Cat in the Hat.

Nobody seemed to know me, everybody passed me by.

I took another close look at her face.

I'd finally met Cat Cassidy. And, man, the girl could really wail.

Under normal circumstances, if I knew I was going to take a guitar solo, I'd warm up a little first. Shake out the fingers. Roll through a couple of licks to limber up the digits. I'd think the song through, the progression, the key we're playing in—get a feel for the tune. Then I'd ease into it, starting slow and steady, focusing on the melody, gradually picking up the speed of my notes and becoming more daring and experimental.

Tonight, I had no such chance.

Cat Cassidy turned to me, giving me a quick once-over. She pointed at her old guitar, and with a big smile on her face shouted, "Do something with it!" and stepped back from the mic as the top of the verse came around again.

Out of nowhere, and just like that, I was thrust into my moment in the sun. I felt all the eyes in the room focus on me, ready to assess my playing, my artistry, and my worthiness to be onstage.

My adrenaline spiked. With the blood rushing in my head, I attacked the neck with all the intensity and confidence of a rock star, only to watch in horror as my fingers froze up and crashed into each other. They looked and felt like four small, paralyzed snakes being dragged over the fretboard. The amplifier behind me emitted a muffled screech as if someone were squashing a parrot in there.

The rhythm section rolled on like nothing had happened. I stopped for a moment and, never taking my eyes off the guitar neck, I shook out my hands and took what women in labor call a deep, cleansing breath. Having no choice but to try again, I flicked the guitar's volume knob all the way up, kicked the amp into overdrive, and jumped back into a blazing solo that caused all the heads on the stage—including Cat's—to nod with approval and, I suspect, relief.

And I have to admit that I was proud of myself, too.

Cat sang one last verse and with the drummer deftly pounding out the last few beats on the snare, we brought the song in for a landing.

As a matter of fact, the drummer had been stomping it pretty good all the way through. He was steady as a rock and filled in from time to time with some nice, fancy stick work. But he was hard to see from where I'd been standing, and I hadn't even tried to get a glimpse of him until that moment. And I almost fell over when I did.

"Timothy!" I shouted.

He shot me a big, toothy grin and a redheaded nod as he counted out the beat to launch us into the next song.

At the office, Timothy had seemed to be a duck out of water. But here onstage he was in the zone, and I jumped right in next to him.

The next several hours felt like a great, melodious dream. We traded songs, solos, and vocals nonstop. When I finally got the chance to survey the crowd, I saw Charles Roland and Plumeria Maple dancing with each other in the middle of the room. It was quite a sight to see, but it wasn't the highlight.

Boogying by himself, twirling and spinning with abandon like a small, bald, caffeinated top, Cal Zander was the star of the dance floor. Everyone was clearly delighted at his enthusiastic, unfettered display of joy.

Onstage, Big Jeff did, indeed, kick butt on the bass. And a guy I hadn't met before did a more than respectable job on the electric keyboard. Needless to say, Gene and Cat's skills on the guitar far outshone my own, and my trying to keep up with them made me a significantly better player by the time the little hand on the clock had swung around to 1:00 a.m. and the crowd began to dissipate.

We played one last song—an old Leadbelly tune called "Goodnight Irene"—before coiling up the cords and shutting down and putting away the equipment and instruments. Everybody pitched in without being asked. A few minutes later, we were all saying good night to one another.

Other than a few shouted words over the music, Cat and I still hadn't talked. We hadn't even been introduced, I realized, so I walked over to her to offer a formal greeting, even though it was obvious that we already knew who each other was.

It was very late, so I really didn't expect to exchange more than a couple of words with Cat. You can imagine my shock when she took me by the hand, led me over to the edge of the stage, and invited me to sit next to her.

"It's the weekend. You a night person, Steve?"

I started to shrug.

"I thought, if you're up to it, if you're not too tired, we could talk a little now. I was sorry I missed you at the office."

I resisted the temptation to look at my watch.

"Well," I said, "I'm pretty sure I can clear my calendar."

Charles Roland and Big Jeff came over to say their good-byes. Both of them offered some nice words about my playing with the group. It felt good, like I'd pulled my weight and made a contribution to the evening.

"Okay, partner," said Big Jeff, embracing Cat in a bear hug. "Be sure to turn out all the lights when you leave, and lock up, and turn on the alarm system, and . . ."

"Can you go over that again?" Cat said with wide-eyed innocence. "Because after all the money I've sunk into this place, I want to be sure I don't forget. Did you say that I should or shouldn't lock the doors?"

Big Jeff gave her a big smooch on the cheek. "Funny girl," he said. "Don't keep her up too late, brah." He patted me on the shoulder and left the room with Charles.

"So, Steve," said Cat, turning to look at me. "I'm so sorry about this afternoon . . ."

She'd set aside the time for me, she explained, but a key client—a Fortune 100 company—had called at the last minute to demand an immediate meeting with the YSC CEO. Not thinking it prudent to blow off a prized account, Cat opted to stand me up instead. A decision I would have made, too, had the roles been reversed.

"Well," I said, trying my best to let her off the hook, "it wasn't a total loss. It did give me a chance to have an interesting talk with your drummer." I watched her reaction. Did she know of Timothy's deep discontent, I wondered?

"I'm sure you got an earful. To be honest, he's not suited for a corporate environment, although he's smart and capable. But it's just not his calling. What you saw him doing tonight," Cat said, looking back at the empty drum set, "is what his real passion is. And to my mind, he should be doing that full-time. So, I'm going to try to help him make that happen."

"So that's your GTY project?" I asked.

"One of them," she said.

"I'd like to hear about how you incorporate Greater Than Yourself into the corporate environment. But it's interesting—in Timothy's case, your offer to help has nothing to do with work. Which is kind of cool, I have to say."

"Thank you for saying so. But that's not entirely true. Timothy earns his paycheck at YSC—he's a hardworking, diligent employee. So he *could* stick around and work for as long as he'd like. But on another level, I think it's poison for him. And it's not really going to help me. Us. His discontent is contagious—no one wants to be around him. And that's tragic. Because, as you saw tonight, when he's in his element, he shines like a nova."

It was true. Watching him tonight was like watching a different person.

"So, it is better for YSC, for our environment at work, to help him to leave. But I want to do it in a way that'll help him to grow. So . . . he's my project. He'll stay where he is for now. But I'm giving him all my contacts in the music world—and I have more than a few—and every opportunity I can to showcase his talent. I'm confident we can hook him up with the right bands, and get him enough studio work to more than match what he makes at YSC. And down the road? Who knows? That'll ultimately be up to him, of course."

"That's incredibly kind of you, Cat. Seriously."

"That's part of what Greater Than Yourself is all about, Steve—seriously." She paused. "It's something you can carry forward to every part of your life. As I'm ultimately going to be doing with Timothy."

"You said that Timothy's one of many projects you're working on. Can you tell me about some of the others?"

"Well," Cat began, "you know by now about my philosophy. When I say *mine,* I mean the philosophy that I've learned from others and adopted myself. I didn't create it. I just try to live by it, because I've experienced firsthand how powerful it is.

"This philosophy—or approach, or methodology—has had a remarkable impact on our company. I can't even begin to tell you the number of employees whose lives have been fundamentally transformed by our Greater Than Yourself environment at YSC. And the value for us? For the business? I don't know that you can put a price tag on the kind of loyalty and commitment our associates have to one another and to our clients. Our turnover is a tenth of the industry average because most people just don't want to leave. Which allows us to put more money into employee development, instead of having to train new people over and over for the same positions. Simply put, our people's commitment is why we're as hot as we are—and their commitment mostly comes from working and living in a GTY culture." Cat paused and considered her words.

"Timothy is a very unusual case," she said, quietly. "But not everyone is suited for our kind of work—his difficulties have nothing to do with Greater Than Yourself, per se. But you've already been hearing about GTY, I understand." She pushed her hair back behind her right ear and smiled.

"Charles has been taking me to school," I said. "He told me that I had to learn about GTY before I could have an audience with you."

"Did he *really*?" Cat burst out in laughter. "He *kills* me," she said, catching her breath. "And you believed him? Wow. You must have thought I was some piece of work."

"Well," I said, hesitating, "the idea intrigued me, so I figured, *Why not? This'll be interesting.*" I could feel my face flushing. Until this moment I'd been convinced that Charles had been speaking for Cat. I felt like a complete doof. And I also felt a whole new level of respect for the scoundrel Roland.

"Okay," she said, putting her hand consolingly on my shoulder. "Either way, I'm glad you've spent time on this. It does represent the core of who I am and what I feel our company's all about."

I gave Cat a quick recap of what I'd learned about the principles of GTY, and whom I'd talked to.

"I've already picked my own first GTY project." I told her about Tommy Spaulding and the new Web site, courtesy of Plumeria Maple.

"So far, though," I said, "I haven't heard a whole lot

about what it means to Give Yourself. I think I have a pretty good idea. But I'd love to hear about it in your own words, if that's alright."

"Of course," said Cat. "It's very simple, really. I can describe the essence of it in three words: *Philanthropize your life.*"

"You made that word up, didn't you?" I said.

"Maybe. But I didn't make up the impulse. Give Yourself is really an act of very personal, one-to-one philanthropy, you know? Look it up in the dictionary. A philanthropist is 'a person who seeks to promote the welfare of others.' Usually we associate it solely with the giving of money to a needy cause, but take the money out of the equation and that's the spirit of Give Yourself. It's the very same impulse, but instead of giving money, you promote another's welfare by opening up the door to your personal inventory and helping them to make the best use of it. And you're not donating to a 'needy cause' so much as to a worthy person."

"Makes sense," I said. "It's a somewhat idealistic view of human nature, but it makes sense."

"I'm not convinced it's so idealistic. You know what gives me a lot of hope, Steve?"

"What's that?"

"The practice of philanthropy is becoming a popular notion. The big boys are helping with that. In 2006, what happened when Warren Buffett pledged to give away eighty-five percent of his forty-billion-dollar fortune to philanthropic foundations?"

"What?"

"It was all over the news. A lot of people thought that unprecedented generosity from arguably the world's greatest moneyman was some kind of contradiction. It was counter-intuitive; therefore, it was newsworthy—and everyone was talking about it."

"True," I said. "A major chunk of that money is going to the Bill & Melinda Gates Foundation."

"Exactly," said Cat. "And then Microsoft announced that Bill Gates would retire to focus on that foundation—to be a full-time philanthropist, in other words.

"Now," she continued, "add to that the popularity of TV shows that build houses for families in need and have competitions to see who can be the biggest giver. It's clear to me that the act of philanthropy has become part of our popular culture. And you know why?"

"Why?"

"Because it appeals to our generosity as human beings. It appeals to our hearts. We're inspired by the stories. Touched by them—because witnessing the act of giving enriches us on a fundamental level. It reminds us that we want our lives to be more than just about ourselves.

"GTY is really just a form of very personal, one-on-one philanthropy. It comes from the same deep impulse, except that you don't have to be rich to undertake it. It's available to everyone. Leave the big money contributions to the Gateses and Buffetts of the world. The rest of us can give our talent, time, knowledge, contacts—whatever resources we have—to other worthy people in our lives at work and at home. We can act, instead of just watching others act or hearing about it in the news.

"To philanthropize your life, then, means first developing a radar of sorts. It's about growing your sensibility to the needs of others and cultivating your desire to promote their welfare, their good or greater fortune, their success, their capacity for achievement."

"Okay, I'm with you," I said. "So, how do I go about doing that?"

"You start with one GTY project, which you've already begun to do. Focusing at first on just one person allows you to concentrate and experiment. You get beyond the concept and right into the application. That's how we learn, by practice. Experimenting. Trial and error. You learned to play guitar that way, didn't you?"

"But what, exactly, do I do for the person who's become my 'project'?"

"You give yourself to that person. Open the floodgates. Invest in that relationship. Give your knowledge. Share your life lessons. Hook them up with your network. Introduce them to the right people. Sing their praises to others. Give them tough, honest feedback and hold them accountable to their commitments. Practice the art of giving, Steve. The art of personal, one-on-one philanthropy. And through that practice you'll examine and discover what works and what doesn't. Put it all under the microscope, as it were, and you'll figure it out, believe me.

"And pretty soon, you'll find that it's more natural than you'd expected. And you'll notice all kinds of GTY opportunities surrounding you. And when you find that there are so many of those opportunities that you're feeling torn about where to devote your energies, you'll know that you've philanthropized your life. And then you'll be in a position to make more of a difference in others' lives than you ever dreamed possible."

"Honestly, Cat?" I said. "That sounds overwhelming. Philanthropize my *life*? I feel torn already, and I haven't even really started on my first project yet. I couldn't possibly devote all my time and energy to others. And, truthfully, I wouldn't want to."

"Neither do I," she said. "Philanthropists don't give to every cause, do they? They educate themselves on what's out there. On who's trying to do what. And then they choose. That's what you need to do, too. Choose."

"Any advice on how to go about doing that?" I asked. "How do you do it?"

She stretched, arching her back. She seemed suddenly tired. And I wondered if the evening was catching up with her. "First of all," she said, "I try to view everyone on my team and in my company as GTY potentials. And I think that everyone is, although they may not be *my* GTYs.

"In other words," she continued, observing the quizzical expression on my face, "everyone's a GTY potential for *someone,* but they may not need exactly what I have to offer. So, I try to facilitate a culture in which everyone reaches out not just to help, but to help each other excel. That's a big part of my job as CEO. In other words, everyone on my team and in our company should become significantly greater as a result of working with one another. And, ideally, they'll all become much better than me at some things, right? My job is to lead the company, not to be the smartest, greatest, most talented person in the building."

"So, your goal is try to surround yourself with people greater than you," I said, trying to finish her thought.

"Close, but that's not exactly what I mean. You're describing the ideal end result, but GTY is a process, it's how we get there. I'm not trying to hire people who are more talented than I am; I'm trying to hire people with heart, desire, drive, and mad potential, and then encourage all of them to bring out the best in one another by giving fully to one another. See the difference?"

I did. "Kind of a mentoring program on steroids, right?"

She pantomimed jabbing a finger down her gagging throat. "Mentoring is not a *program*. You can't assign the roles of mentor and mentee and then expect something great to happen. In essence, GTY is an act of love. You can't assign that; you have to encourage it. Don't get me wrong. There are some truly exceptional community, school, and faith-based mentoring programs around the world. And I say, God bless them, more power to them, have at it. And there are some— and I mean some—good corporate programs. Kudos to them, too. For the most part, though, they just don't take it far enough.

"Imagine this, Steve. Instead of assigning, say, each member of a senior management team one junior person to 'mentor' as a part of a program or initiative, you build a culture that encourages—and ultimately expects—everyone to engage in the act of giving to someone all the time. That's no program. That's magic."

"Is that what YSC is like?" I asked, thinking of Timothy.

"We're not there yet," she admitted. "And maybe we'll never get there. But the attempt itself is worth it.

"And if I'm being honest, this isn't always going to work with every person. The reality is that we're all flawed in our own ways, right? And, frankly, there are people out there who are *significantly* messed up in some really, *really* fundamental ways. Some people are deeply apathetic about anything except their own self-interest. Some are psychotic. Some people are just mean or obnoxious or—whatever. But in my experience, I've just described a very small minority of people."

She paused, almost seeming to lose her composure.

"The vast majority of people want to grow, to thrive, to contribute, to make a difference. Those are the people I want to encourage, to cultivate, to build and expand my company around. I'm not going to operate my business based on the lowest common denominator. I'm going to do whatever I can to cultivate the philanthropic impulse that exists in most people."

This is a woman I could work for, I thought. And believe me, I can count on one hand how many times I've had *that* feeling about another person over the years. And I've met more than my fair share of fair-haired CEOs.

"The best way I can encourage others is, of course, by my own example," Cat continued. "So in addition to looking out for the company as a whole, I'm always on the lookout for my own GTY projects—for those individuals who can benefit from me in a significant way. I'm always looking for someone I can personally invest in, someone who'll grow specifically from what I have to offer."

"Do you mean that you're looking for that person who'll be your eventual replacement?"

"Always. Of course. But mostly I'm looking for someone who could skyrocket with the right boost, input, or support from me. I look for someone with a combination of potential, desire, work ethic, drive, and heart. Someone I deeply believe in. They may or may not end up replacing me as CEO—but they will surpass my skills and talents in some arena, from marketing to number crunching, strategic thinking or communication skills. I'm pretty well-rounded and at least adequate in all those areas—a CEO has to be. But if I can help someone on my team become, for example, a marketing rock star—an industry legend—then I'm really doing my job."

"That's great, Cat. It really is," I said. "But not all of us are CEO material."

"Doesn't matter." She yawned, giving further evidence that the late hour was taking its toll. "Everyone should take the same approach. Say I'm an IT manager. I should want my techs to end up setting a new standard for the industry, and I do that not by promoting and aggrandizing myself, but by GTYing the right people on my team and shining a spotlight on them and their teammates. Ditto for sales, purchasing, finance, HR—you name it."

"Okay," I relented, "I don't have to be the CEO. I could be in any position of leadership."

"Frankly, Steve?" said Cat. "You're still not getting what I mean by 'everyone.' "

"Okay . . ." I said. "So this isn't just a management practice?"

"Right." She smiled. "I started looking for my own GTY projects from the moment I got a job as an intern at YSC. Just because I worked for somebody else didn't mean I had nothing to give. And why shouldn't I try to make one of my peers greater than myself?" she insisted. "Or my boss? This isn't about your position or title, it's about your human beingness. There should be no limitations, and it should never, ever stop."

I thought again about Tommy and my own Project Spaulding. Who else, in addition to Tommy, could I choose to help? And as several candidates sprung immediately to mind, something inside me twinged.

"Cat," I said, hearing a touch of angst in my own voice, "where do you get the time for this? How can you possibly give like that all the time, and to so many people? When do you have time for yourself? How do you run the company? How do you keep from being overwhelmed?"

"Whoa!" she said, laughing, interrupting me with a raise of her hand. "That's a lot of questions. But there's really one easy answer."

She paused, exhibiting a flair for the dramatic while she watched the anticipation build on my face.

"I tithe."

"You what?"

"You know. Tithing. Usually it means that you take a percentage of your income—say ten percent—and donate it regularly to your place of worship or charity or organization."

"Yes," I said, a little irritated, "I know what tithing is."

"Well, same thing. Except I'm talking about time instead of money. I tithe a percentage of my time to my GTY projects. I figure I work somewhere between sixty and seventy hours a week; if I'm tithing ten percent of my time, I'm devoting six to seven hours a week to my GTY projects. Usually, that's plenty. And if I'm maxed out, I don't take on any more until my time frees up. You can tithe more or less; you can base it on working hours, leisure hours, or waking hours, if you want. It's entirely up to you—the key is to find the time allocation that works for you, and then to be consistent. You may choose to put all your time-tithe into one project— especially at first—or spread it out over several. Again, it's up to you. It's your time, after all."

I sat in silence for a moment while I let the idea sink in. I tried to summon my devil's advocate, who's usually perched on my shoulder by this time, anxiously prodding me to shoot holes in the concept at hand. But he didn't appear. The time-tithe was a simple and elegant solution.

"So, Cat," I said, coming back to something she'd said a few minutes earlier. "When you first started at YSC—when you were an intern—did you ever choose one of your bosses as a GTY project?"

She laughed.

"Oh, yes indeedy. I did."

"And what happened?" I asked.

"I happened," said the CEO.

I sat on the stage as Cat dashed around the room flipping light switches until the only illumination left was the red exit sign over the door behind the stage. We gathered up our guitars and then Cat opened a panel next to the door and armed the alarm system, as Big Jeff had told her to do. We pushed through the door and out into the bracing late night/early morning air.

Since my car was parked on the other side of the building in the strip mall, Cat's hybrid SUV was the only vehicle out here. I, gentleman that I am, walked her to her car.

"Hey, Cat," I said as she stowed her guitar in the back, "why don't you keep this for the rest of the weekend?" I slid my guitar in next to hers.

She looked at me, surprised.

"You loved this guitar, right? You never really wanted to sell it. I'm sure you never expected to see it again. So . . . go on. Take it, play it a little."

She gave me a hug.

"Thank you," she said, a little choked up. "I didn't want to ask . . ."

"Glad to do it," I said. "And thank you for being so generous with your time tonight. Don't get me wrong, the jam session was awesome. But our conversation was the real treasure for me. I have a lot to think about—which is a good thing, right?"

"Yes." She laughed.

She opened the driver's side door, slid behind the wheel, and turned the key while I held the door open.

"In fact," Cat said, "you may want to consider doing what I do."

"What's that?"

"I carve out one evening a week—Sundays, usually—to sit by myself or with someone I trust—and think. I think about the week I've left behind and the one ahead. I have no agenda. It's not a planning session. I just think. Reflect. You wouldn't believe the clarity that can come out of it. I usually go to Caledonia Mission in San Diego. It's always open and usually empty. Something about the old stone and wood makes me feel at peace. That's my special place. You may have one, too. A place that gives you peace?"

I didn't.

"Anyway"—she reached for the door handle—"I need to get on the road before I get too sleepy. Come by the office sometime next week and we can talk some more."

"Yeah, sure. I'd love to. It's got to be better than my last office visit."

She laughed again. "You'll never let me live that down, will you?"

"Not a chance," I said as I closed her door and waved.

She pulled away and I headed back to my own car. I felt really good about lending her the old Gibson. I stuffed my cold hands into my pockets as I began to walk. And in there I felt a familiar piece of folded paper.

I turned to shout to Cat, waving the note in the air as I tried to catch her attention. But it was too late. I watched her taillights disappear down Poway Road.

This was ridiculous already. For all I knew, she still didn't know this note existed—and that just wasn't right. I was going to have to do something about that, and sooner rather than later. And to be certain that Cat and her note wouldn't miss each other again, I was determined to put it into her hands myself. And suddenly it dawned on me exactly when and where that delivery should take place.

Caledonia Mission was nestled at the end of a shady street in the Old Town neighborhood of San Diego. I parked my car down the street next to a Mexican restaurant and walked up the sidewalk toward the old Spanish building with the white plaster exterior. The multitiered bell tower caught shadows cast by the streetlights, which had recently turned themselves on in response to the darkness of this late Sunday evening. The lush landscaping of agave, palms, and desert flowers in full bloom gave off a deep sense of tranquility as I walked on a stone path leading to the garden gate. I fully expected it to be locked for the night. I nearly lost my footing as it swung easily open, and I all but flew up the steps toward the giant, hardwood double doors.

I stepped quietly into the rustic, dimly lit chapel and saw a few silhouettes scattered among the austere pews. Nobody turned to look at me, so I was faced with the task of trying to sort out which of these people, if any, was Cat. After all, she didn't say she came here every Sunday night—and even if she did come tonight, I was completely rolling the dice as to the time.

I sat in a pew a few rows from the back and tried to relax. I closed my eyes, and within minutes I nodded off into a pleasant, dreamless doze.

I don't know how much time had gone by, but I awoke with a start, stretched, and looked around. As far as I could tell, there were only two of us left in the sanctuary. The other person was a few rows in front of me, so I stood up and walked down the center aisle planning to cop an inconspicuous glance at the person's face in the unlikely event that it belonged to Cat. And unfortunately, it didn't.

Disappointed but not surprised, I turned and walked back toward the door.

I heard the astonished whisper even before my brain figured out what was being said.

"Steve? Is that you?"

My heart jumped. It was Cat. She was sitting in the darkness on the other side of the aisle, a couple of rows back from where I'd been . . . um . . . reflecting.

"What are you doing here?" she whispered.

Encouraged by the fact that she sounded more pleased than stalked, I walked over and sat down next to her.

"Looking for you," I said.

Although she still didn't fit my image of a high-powered CEO, she was dressed a little less rocker-ish than she had been on Friday night at the Mullet, wearing some kind of a pants suit and—more to the point—shoes.

"Really? Why?" she asked.

I handed her the note.

"Did Charles or Gene tell you about this?" I asked.

She looked at the folded paper. "About what?"

"Go ahead," I said. "Read it."

I watched her face as she did. I was curious what, if any, emotion would show. Let's put it this way: She'd be a terrible poker player. Within seconds, I saw traces of shock, love, remorse, gratitude, and lord knows what else pass across her petite features like colored lights through a prism.

"How . . . how did you get this?" A tear rolled down her face and disappeared down her neck.

"It was in my . . . your guitar case. I found it in there. That's what started me on my Greater Than Yourself excursion. I was going to give it to you at your office. And then the other night, but I didn't remember the note until after you'd gone. So . . . here I am. Mission accomplished," I said as I motioned to our surroundings to drive home the dopey pun.

She leaned over and kissed my cheek.

"I can't believe your boy, Charles, didn't tell you about it." I admonished him in absentia.

"Oh . . . it was much, much better this way! Don't you think?" said a voice from behind me.

I jumped up and spun around. There was Charles himself.

"What the hell, Charles?" I cried.

He put a finger to his lips. "Language, Steve. Remember where we are. Use your indoor voice, please."

Cat and Charles enjoyed a good laugh at my expense.

"Do you always follow your boss around town?" I said.

"Look who's talking about following," he said, grinning.

"Charles often meets me here on Sunday nights," said Cat. "And, just so you know, Steve, he's most certainly not following his boss around."

"Okay, okay," I said. "He's not following you."

"What I mean," said Cat, "is that I'm not Charles's boss."

"You're not?"

"No." She laughed. "Quite the contrary."

"I'm not tracking," I said, confused.

"Let's start over," said Cat. "Steve, I'd like you to meet Charles Roland, founder and chairman of YSC Corporation."

"Charmed, I'm sure," said Charles, holding out his hand.

I'm rarely the one who's at a loss for words. Usually, my first response to an unexpected turn of events is to let loose an array of cutting witticisms.

This time was an exception. I was literally struck dumb.

"Allow me to explain," said Charles with far too much glee. "Cat Cassidy is an example of the third GTY principle called, as you know, Replicate Yourself. She was my GTY project almost from the moment she first walked through our doors at YSC. Back then, as the CEO, I used to give the new-employee orientations where I'd explain our work, values, and vision."

"And he'd talk about GTY," said Cat. "This is all Charles's language, you know." She chuckled, having even more fun with this than Charles. "And on our first day of work, he challenged each of us to seek out our own Greater Than Yourself projects.

"'You want to get noticed around here?' he'd say. 'Then use your life experience to start raising someone else up.' I still remember it."

"Yes, you do," said Charles. "I heard you give the same talk to our new recruits just last week.

"Cat was a Greater Than Yourself phenom from the get-go. She'd been with us for less than a month when one day she came into my office and announced that I'd be her first project. She told me that she was a great communicator and that I could learn a lot from her if I'd let her help. And she was right. Except for my little orientation speech, which I'd done a million times, communication had always been a major weakness of mine."

"But not anymore," said Cat.

"No, not anymore."

"You were Cat's project?" I said, regaining a modicum of composure.

"Only at first," Cat explained.

"Right," agreed Charles. "I turned the tables on her pretty quickly. I saw qualities in her that she had no idea she possessed. I saw my successor. And in ten or so years, that's exactly what she became. She's grown into a better CEO than I ever was. So I stepped aside, kept my chairman position, and assumed more of an advisory role. Now, I'm just here to be of service."

"You replicated yourself," I said.

"Exactly," said Charles. "But not because she's just like me—we're very different in a lot of ways. And it's not because she took over as CEO."

"He was replicating the act of Greater Than Yourself through me," Cat said. "His investment in me, generous as it was, wasn't completely unconditional. He attached one non-negotiable rider to our relationship. The one thing that Charles expected from me as a kind of repayment for his services was that I would make a practice of finding my own Greater Than Yourself projects, too. And that the people I GTYed would be obligated to find their own projects, and so on and so forth all the way down the line."

"That's the One Condition of GTY," Charles reiterated. "That you do the same for someone else. Pay it forward, and demand that those you teach pay it forward as well."

"To infinity," I said.

"I'll drink to that," said Charles.

As he stood, I looked at him anew. Now that I thought about Charles, I should have seen that he was more than he seemed from our first encounter. Charles always had an air of confidence and self-assurance about him. Contentment. He gave off a nearly palpable sense of accomplishment and success. He was also just so *likeable*. I recalled Big Jeff's story of little Chucky's childhood epiphany. Now it all made perfect sense.

"So, Charles—or should I say Chucky?" I said as Cat and I stood. "YSC was the fulfillment of your sixth-grade dream? I guess owning the hottest staffing and executive placement firm in the industry is a pretty good way to help others achieve their dreams, isn't it?"

"Yes, it is. Funny you should make that connection."

"Why's that?" I said.

"The name of the company is actually my backhanded tribute to those middle-school tormenters who ridiculed me for my dream. I guess it's my way of thumbing my nose at them."

"How so?" I asked.

"It has to do with what the acronym YSC stands for, Steve," said Cat.

"Okay," I said. "What does it stand for?"

Cat and Charles looked conspiratorially at each other.

"Well, my friend," said Charles, "only a very few know the full name behind the initials—and the childhood history that stands behind it. Someone once said that success is the best revenge. And so I named my own company after myself."

"Wait," I said, as it slowly dawned on me. "You have got to be kidding. The name of your company is You Suck Chuck?"

"Bingo," said Charles Roland.

As funny as I thought that was, I can't say I was terribly surprised by the ironic humor. It was Charles's brand. It had only been a few days since we'd met, but I already felt like I'd known him for ages. Maybe it's because he'd taught me something so significant.

Yes. *He'd* taught me.

It was clear to me now that since our very first meeting at the coffee shop, Charles had intentionally and purposefully facilitated my learning excursion into the world of Greater Than Yourself. He pushed the credit to others along the way. Plumeria, Gene, Big Jeff, Cat—they were always presented as the stars, the experts. Never Charles.

But he was the one who made it happen, who nudged me along. He gave me his insight, his time and attention. And he connected me with his friends, never asking for anything in return. And now I knew why.

I don't know why he saw me as a worthy recipient. It seemed too good to be true. But there was no denying it.

I was Charles Roland's latest GTY project.

As we walked up the aisle toward the exit of Caledonia

Mission, I looked in awe at my two incredible companions. For some reason, they'd enlisted me to help carry the torch of Greater Than Yourself. And I didn't want to let them down.

What was I supposed to do now? *I'll figure it out,* I told myself. With a little help from my friends.

And then, only a few short days after my fateful purchase of that beautiful, old guitar, Charles Roland, Cat Cassidy, and I left the chapel together and walked out silently into the night.

I'm honored that you've stayed with me throughout the telling of this story. I hope it has opened your eyes to the Greater Than Yourself philosophy, and has made you think. But, as you may recall, there are strings attached to this journey. Obligations. Serious ones. And that, my reader friend, is where you come in. As a matter of fact, you're the strings. Not long ago, I made a vow that I would practice Greater Than Yourself before I'd preach about it. Remember? Sure you do. Back on page 34.

There was one thing I neglected to mention at the time, though. It has to do with what you now know as the principle called Replicate Yourself.

So, here's the deal:

Consider for a moment that by virtue of your reading this story, you are—in effect—my GTY project. I don't know that that line of reasoning would stand up in a court of law, but I think I could make a reasonable case for the logic of it. Are you with me on that?

Good.

As you know, there is the matter of the "one condition," as Charles and Cat called it.

So, you know what that means:

It's time for *you* to choose a GTY project, too.

What follows on the next pages are the tools you can use to get the process started, as well as a documented case study of Greater Than Yourself in action to help you generate your own ideas on how to carry this forward.

No excuses necessary, my friend. Let's change the world, you and I, shall we?

One person at a time . . .

Starting with you.

In January 2008, while the story you've just read was still being written, I gave a speech to the new students and staff of the Up with People program. They were around a hundred people, ages eighteen through twenty-nine, from twenty-three different countries, who were about to set out on a tour that would take them through the United States, Mexico, and Thailand.

I talked about Extreme Leadership. About taking on the challenge to change the world for the better. My usual stuff.

And then, unrehearsed, and more or less off the top of my head, I spoke to them about Greater Than Yourself. I had never talked to any group or audience about the ideas contained within this book, and, frankly, I was still sorting a lot of this out for myself.

Nonetheless, I challenged all of them to practice the tenets of Expand Yourself, Give Yourself, and Replicate Yourself as they traveled the globe, worked in local communities, stayed with host families, and learned about one another over the coming six months.

I wasn't very specific. Or prescriptive. I figured they'd figure it out for themselves. I encouraged them to stay in touch with me and share their GTY stories. I would be standing by, ready to help with advice and counsel.

Nothing happened.

So, I tried again.

This time, I went to the sixteen staff members—the Up with People employees responsible for facilitating a great experience for the student participants—and I made the challenge very specific: that each of them should take on one person as their GTY Project. Still, I didn't prescribe what they should do or how they should do it. I just urged them to try.

That's when the magic happened.

Staff member Andrew Lanham, who was kind enough to document the experiment, wrote the following account of their subsequent experience and the lessons they learned from it.

EPILOGUE
by Andrew Lanham

The Greater Than Yourself challenge landed on the table with a thud. For starters, any brand-new, semi-time-consuming project presented to the sixteen men and women who make up the staff of an Up with People cast has to overcome a lot of obstacles to be approved.

Up with People is an international education program that uses music as a way to communicate and inspire others. It offers students over the course of a six-month program first-hand exposure to social issues and local needs all over the world. Each staff member in an Up with People cast has a very specific job title: education, logistics, finance, dance, technical, et cetera. Cast members serve the education and development of 110 students, between the ages of eighteen and twenty-nine, from twenty-nine different countries—while traveling *around the world*. In addition, every staff member helps his or her coworkers in achieving the requirements of their jobs. In Up with People, before you even start a new task, you feel as if your time has already been completely consumed.

Moreover, wasn't this Greater Than Yourself initiative a little rough around the edges? It sounded almost new age-y—to "replicate yourself"?

Martin Brennan, the manager of our cast (the term we use to describe our employees and the students traveling in our program), asked who on our staff felt uncomfortable with the challenge. Over half of the sixteen staff members lifted their hands.

In the Greater Than Yourself challenge, each of the sixteen staff members was asked to take on his or her own individual GTY project over the last seven weeks of the January–June, six-month Up with People tour. The challenge was received with hesitation and reluctance, at first.

But what happened next was truly extraordinary.

THE WORK of elevating those around you, and thereby raising yourself up in the process, is a dream that most would readily subscribe to. But it is an exercise that few are familiar with.

There are a number of key words that crop up in the course of implementing GTY: *greatness, ability, expansion, knowledge, perspective, experience, give.* They are words and concepts one assumes are already part of our daily lives. They inspire this kind of familiarity because they *should* be part of our working lives; this is how they are intended. Through GTY, however, we quickly realized that these words were noticeably absent from our vocabulary and daily walk.

One tricky part of a Greater Than Yourself project is that you cannot truly give in a worthwhile way to those around you without accepting within yourself the qualities the program emphasizes. You must be willing to expand yourself, to give of your abilities to another, to tap into the greatness inherent not only in you, but in those around you.

A number of our staff bristled at being asked to begin a

formal GTY project. Our staff is made up of an uncommonly generous and giving group of people, by anyone's measure. Up with People employees are hired not just for their ability to do the job, but also for their willingness to help guide the students around them. In one regard this makes Up with People the perfect place to put Greater Than Yourself into action. Where better to test GTY than in an environment where the staff members are already *required* to work daily with some of GTY's key principles?

However, Up with People is also a challenging business with which to integrate GTY. The staff members of Up with People want to believe that the Golden Rule is already at work in our lives regardless of whether we specifically embrace a GTY project. They believe it is human nature. Having to bring GTY into our lives and workplace demonstrated that, without *intentionality,* the Golden Rule is nothing but an optimist's dream.

To successfully incorporate GTY, one must wholeheartedly embrace philanthropy and the elevation of others in daily life. GTY is a road map toward putting the Golden Rule into action. It is about transforming a workplace into a culture of giving.

At the beginning of the GTY challenge, many of us felt that we were already doing what was being asked of us, and to put the GTY name to it would falsify our actions. Many of us simply did not know how we felt about the GTY challenge. But one of the great fundamental truths we learned from GTY is that the simple action of raising one individual to a place he or she had only hoped to reach is the essence of inspiration itself.

This will be challenging at first, just as all worthwhile endeavors are. We discovered that one's first GTY project at times feels as frustrating as the first time one exercises after years spent sitting on the couch. Working on your first project feels like you are growing a new muscle in a place where you're not even sure muscle is supposed to exist.

As we discovered, there are GTY projects all around us waiting for the specific vision and gifts that *only we* can provide. What follows are some of the observations and results that the Up with People staff experienced in tackling the Greater Than Yourself challenge.

FOLAJIMI "Fola" Akinyemi grew up just outside of Denver, Colorado, where Up with People has its headquarters. At the beginning of her first semester, by her own admission, Fola was "annoying, abrasive, loud, and filled with self-doubt about my ability to talk to others and be accepted."

Aoife Valerie Redmond was raised an ocean away in a small village in Ireland, and had been traveling as an education coordinator with Up with People for a year and a half. Aoife was one of the more outspoken staff members; she voiced opposition to GTY at the beginning of the challenge. She felt the people around her already exemplified GTY without putting "needless labels" on it. She also felt that to tell someone else they were her GTY project would insult them and flaunt her own abilities.

To overcome her initial hesitation, Aoife approached Fola almost immediately after the challenge was announced and told her, in typically blunt fashion, that Fola had always annoyed her. Despite this, Aoife said, Fola had come a long way, and Aoife was proud of all the work she had done toward bettering herself. Would she like to be Aoife's GTY project and "maybe talk about what other work she can start on to prepare for life back home?"

Fola immediately said yes; she was "flattered beyond belief."

One common concern among our staff's efforts to initiate GTY projects was their unease at the very idea of asking someone to be a GTY project. Scott Enebo, our assistant cast manager from the United States, thought at first that it "just felt false."

Scott chose Ultan Courtney, from Dublin, Ireland, as his project. Ultan described what was a similar reaction to *every person* who was asked to be a GTY project.

"It just felt amazing," he said. "The very act of Scott coming up to me and saying, 'Hey, I see some really great qualities in you, but I think maybe you're holding yourself back a little. Would you like to sit down and have some chats and see if I can't help you get to where you want to be?' It made me want to say yes, just lifted me right up. It starts you off at a place where you feel like you can go somewhere, because someone with more experience sees the potential in you for something great."

FOUR OF our sixteen staff members chose not to pursue the GTY challenge, unable to get past their initial hesitation. The rest soon discovered a constant element in GTY projects— always expect the unexpected.

NOT EVERY GTY project can be a success. A number of our staff's projects either failed to get off the ground or started with great intensity but quickly died out. In order to ensure success with a project, you must follow the steps laid out in this book.

The goals of a GTY project can be as wide-ranging as you wish—the challenge itself allows for a great deal of flexibility and freedom in both its design and execution. You can choose *anyone* as your GTY project, and you and the person who is your project can work on *anything*. Within the project itself there are few specific rules to follow. This, however, makes it all too easy to *not* follow the few steps that are laid out.

Before starting a project you must be sure that you have fully considered whom you are choosing. Maria Fahlin, our vocal coordinator from Sweden, chose her coworker, dance captain Yui Mihara, from Japan. Yui plans to move to Sweden in a year and a half and Maria felt that she could help guide Yui during this transition. But because Yui's planned move was so far away, their GTY project never got off the ground. We discovered it is important to pick a person as a GTY project who is able to improve from your gifts *right now*, not someone who may not be ready to do so until sometime in the future.

Yui chose her intern, Astrid Vargas, from Mexico, as her GTY project. They started off wonderfully because they had a close working relationship. If you are in a position to choose someone you already work closely with as your initial GTY project, that can be a plus. It is important to have a trusting relationship with the person who is your project to ensure success. Unfortunately, the majority of our six-week GTY challenge occurred in Thailand, where time together and Yui's job responsibilities as dance captain made getting together more difficult.

This is not to say that Yui and Astrid's project was a total failure—they had some good discussions about how Astrid could improve her dancing techniques and speak in front of and lead large groups of people. But we discovered you must consider the element of time in choosing your GTY project— not just your ability to tithe your own time (you should consider this before even making the commitment to take on a GTY project), but your ability to have time alone with the other person to actually do the work needed.

You must also both be fully dedicated to the GTY challenge before starting your project. Gabe Anchondo, our show manager, who grew up surrounded by performance experience in Tucson, Arizona, chose Micha Radner as his project without ever specifically telling Micha that their work together would be a GTY project. Gabe knew of Micha's desire to better understand theater production and told Micha that he could shadow him during workdays.

Three weeks into the project, Micha had gained a great deal of experience and knowledge. He told us, "Working with Gabe has been so incredible. Before, I thought I would just go home to Germany after Up with People and work there. Now that Gabe has shown this interest in me, I realize how much I have learned these past six months. I think that working with Gabe has given me the courage to move out of my hometown when I get back and start a new life, the kind of life that I want."

Despite this, Gabe was never fully comfortable with the concept of GTY. As a result, he was never able to truly commit to the project. Because of this reluctance on his part, Gabe was convinced that he had not made much progress with Micha, and their project did not move forward farther after this early peak.

Gabe and Micha stand as proof that there are rewards to be found in undertaking a GTY project even when it is not a complete success. How much farther would they have been able to go, however, if Gabe had embraced the GTY challenge fully and discussed it openly with Micha? In choosing a GTY project, you must be clear on what the challenge itself entails. There must be open communication between you and the person who is your project to hold each other accountable on the road to success.

Ellen Enebo, our education manager, chose Mitch McVicker, an education coordinator who works under her, as her GTY project. She chose Mitch because she felt she could help him learn how to improve his use of Excel spreadsheets, thereby increasing the efficiency with which he is able to do his job. Also, Ellen and Mitch are both from the United States, and will therefore continue the use of Excel in their respective jobs after leaving Up with People. Ellen and Mitch achieved their goal, but their GTY project lasted only one week and failed to move forward to higher goals.

As we learned, in choosing your *first* GTY project, it is important to set high enough goals to expand both yourself and the other person. Later, once you have mastered the concepts of GTY, and you see how GTY changes things in small ways throughout your life and work, it is possible to undertake smaller, less time-consuming GTY projects.

For one's first project, however, it is important to reach for the realm of masters that Steve Farber talks about in this book, the place where you elevate those around you to be the very best at what they do, and through this raise yourself up to the highest, most respected level of all.

IT IS EASY, during your first GTY project, to question whether things are going well. Something that deals so closely with deep, personal truths—"Where am I going? How can I best use my abilities to get there?"—can be hard to talk openly about at first. It helps to have others outside of your project to talk with.

Scott Enebo found it helpful to discuss how things were going with his wife, Ellen.

"I share all of my struggles and triumphs with her," Scott said. "I don't tell her Ultan's personal information, but I discuss things with her, ask her for advice. If things aren't going well, she's there to give me a different perspective."

We found having an outside perspective is key to GTY's success. You are, after all, asking the person who is your project to develop new perspectives on life—so you must do the same.

Wouter Oosterheert, our logistics coordinator from The Netherlands, was immediately taken with the principles of GTY.

"It's just such a wonderful idea," he said. "It takes concepts we're all already thinking about and puts them into action to help others, and in doing that, you help yourself. Who wouldn't want to be a part of everyone becoming something better than they are already?"

Despite this, Wouter had a hard time getting his project off the ground. He initially decided to ask his former intern to work with him. Unfortunately, when he made this decision she was away, applying to graduate schools. When she returned, the cast immediately began its three-day marathon trip to Thailand, at which point Wouter went off with seven students to live with an indigenous hill tribe for a week.

Halfway through that week, Wouter realized he had only two and a half weeks left to complete his project and he hadn't even begun. He asked a number of staff members for their input on what he should do.

"If I had already spoken with my previous intern," Wouter said, "then I would have moved forward and just made the best of it. But since I never spoke with her, I decided to ask my new intern, Sofie, if she would work with me. I knew we didn't have much time, but at least with Sofie we'd be together every day for the last two weeks. I decided not to give up and just put my all into it."

Sofie Martinsson is a highly intelligent twenty-four-year-old woman from Sweden who had difficulties balancing her desire to please those around her with meeting her own needs. Given her incredible work ethic, Sofie had developed an almost complete inability to set goals for herself.

With only two and a half weeks to work together, Wouter threw himself into his GTY project with total abandon. Sofie, never having had anyone with which to discuss her fears of moving back home, suddenly had an hour each day to discuss her future plans with Wouter.

Wouter started by taking inventory, not only for Sofie, but himself as well. What are your talents, passions, fears, hopes, goals? He then gave Sofie reading material on goal setting and work-performance skills. He provided her with tests designed to help push you toward discovering where you want to go in life. He had Sofie describe herself at length, how she felt she had become the way she was, and what about herself she wished to change.

Two weeks into their project, three days before the end of the semester, Sofie came to Wouter with a broad smile across her face.

"I did it," she said. "I'm greater than you at goal setting!"

From across the lake, others could see the six-foot-four Wouter Oosterheert jumping up and down in delight.

"All of a sudden everything just clicked," Sofie later said. "Wouter gave me a book to read on visualizing your goals and suddenly I just got it. It was like all this time I'd been having thoughts and not knowing where to go with them and suddenly this man comes along and . . . makes me see the potential in myself. I now have goals, real goals that work for me, and I know how I'm going to achieve these goals. As soon as I get home I want to start my own GTY project, I want to use GTY in my life. It's like when a teacher sees something special in you in school—only it's out in the real world where it means so much more."

Wouter achieved this with Sofie in two and a half weeks; imagine what could be accomplished with more time.

"The best part," Wouter said, "was that moment when Sophie said she was greater than me. But what was also so amazing was that, in that moment, I realized how much I had learned about myself. In Up with People I had wanted to work on improving my interactions with others, and now, here, I had finally learned to do that. The greatest thing about GTY is that it allows you to examine what your strengths are. It doesn't ask you to spend your time thinking about what you *can't* do. It finds your strengths and improves upon them."

ALL OF THE GTY projects that enjoyed the kind of reciprocal energy that Wouter and Sofie experienced were successful in similar ways.

Martin Brennan, our cast manager, created a year-long plan that will continue in the coming months to help make David Penny, our admissions coordinator, a better public speaker. Martin and David have the advantage, in this long-term plan, of living relatively close to each other in the United States, where they are from.

"I now feel," David said, "like I know for the first time how to demonstrate the passion I have when speaking in front of groups. I wouldn't be at this place in my public speaking abilities without GTY."

Celiana Dolovitz, our business manager from Venezuela, watched her GTY project, Molly Robertson, who grew up in San Francisco, receive a job on staff with Up with People for the upcoming semester.

"Just working so closely with me was amazing," Molly said. "I feel like if I'd had a mentor it would have been so much different. This was as natural as a friendship, only with the intention of raising me up. That's so rewarding."

Scott, who struggled throughout his project to find adequate time to meet with Ultan, eventually sat down with him for a marathon two-hour discussion.

"I just felt directionless," Ultan said. "GTY has pointed me toward where I want to go."

Aoife spent so much time working with Fola that, by the end of the semester, they referred to each other as "sister."

"Fola," Aoife said, "who used to just drive me up a wall she was so annoying, is my friend now, my kid sister. But I don't think it was me who made her better. I don't really think I had much to do with it at all. It was all Fola, she did the work. I only listened and put my two cents in every so often."

Fola sees things differently.

"Aoife choosing me as her GTY project has changed my life. I mean, I don't want to make it sound like too big of a deal. But in a way it is. I know I grew a lot over this year. A whole lot! But I don't think I would have been able to really see that without Aoife and GTY's help. It's one thing to learn and expand, but GTY is what made me see *how* that had happened, and more importantly, how it can *continue* to happen. It helped me put things into practice so they won't ever fade away."

Aoife made one radical choice that no other staff member made. She gave Fola the assignment of finding her own GTY project the very first time they met together.

"I chose this girl who really annoyed me," Fola says, laughing. "Because I figured it must be the same way that I annoyed Aoife when we met! I just talked more with her, made the effort to be her friend, and then tried to help her. I worked with her to practice looking people in the eyes when she talked, to show confidence. And it was funny, everything we worked on, I realized I was improving in myself. And I realized there's something to respect and cherish in everyone."

"I just knew," Aoife says, "that it should always be about Fola, she's the project. But giving her a GTY project as well would put what I helped her with into practice. Otherwise where does it go?"

So Aoife chose to replicate herself with Fola immediately. In the other successful projects this happened naturally and organically at the project's conclusion. We found that to have a successful GTY project, you must take steps to make the project your own. GTY not only allows for this, but demands it.

AT THE END of every semester, we have a final banquet dinner for our staff. During this dinner it is a tradition to have sixteen surprise guests. One student, who has a special relationship with a specific staff member, is allowed into the room to read an appreciation letter he or she has written about this staff member. The students call this "Project Make-'Um-Cry."

During our final staff banquet, ten of the sixteen students who spoke mentioned Greater Than Yourself. Only six of these students were actual GTY projects. Again and again we heard the refrain, "Because of you, I am greater than I was."

It was a beautiful, amazing thing to watch GTY spread across a workplace, across lives. You start to notice GTY happening in small instances everywhere you look. You start to talk with your close friends and coworkers about how you can help one another in ways you never would have before. The rising greatness of all becomes a reality.

It starts with you choosing one project. Your project must then choose his or her own project. In this way, GTY grows naturally all around you. What results from all of this is that GTY becomes not just a challenge, but a culture. A living, breathing culture of greatness, as everyone benefits.

Greater Than Yourself has the power to change the world.

All you have to do is take the first step. Look around you now. Whom can you help? Imagine if the person beside you was thinking the very same thing. It's right there, within your grasp; all you have to do is choose.

So, what are you waiting for?

GREATER THAN YOURSELF

A Framework for Action

> *"Your job is to extend and offer yourself to
> another, with the express purpose of elevating
> that person above yourself."*
> —Charles Roland

A vow is not something to take lightly. But with Greater Than
Yourself, there is no preaching without the practice; no saying without doing. Here is a framework to help you commit
to a Greater Than Yourself vow of your own.

EXPAND YOURSELF

> *"Self-expansion is a perpetual enterprise. And
> because it's the foundation of whatever you
> do for others, expanding yourself is the fur-
> thest thing from selfishness. You expand
> yourself in order to give yourself to others."*
> —Plumeria Maple

I will create a deep and expansive sense of who I am (so that
eventually I can give it all away) by doing the following:

1. Shifting my perception about myself:
   - Isolation   →   Connection
   - Alone   →   Interdependent
   - Me   →   Us

2. Taking a personal inventory of:
   - Things I do well
   - Meaningful experiences I have had
   - Life lessons I have learned
   - People I know
   - My admirable qualities
   - My personal values

3. Asking myself:
   - Is what I am currently doing helping me to:
     a. Expand on the items that are already in my inventory?
     b. Add to my inventory?
     c. Deepen my mastery and wisdom?
   - What more can I do to improve the quality and depth of my experience and knowledge?

4. Choosing my GTY project wisely
   - Focus on someone:
     a. Whom I trust
     b. Whom I believe in
     c. Who can benefit from and improve upon my gifts
     d. Who has the drive, energy, heart, and desire to take full advantage of what I give them

  e. Whose values are congruent with my own
  f. Who has qualities and abilities I admire
  g. Whom I love or care deeply about

GIVE YOURSELF

> "*Leave the big-money contributions to the
> Gateses and Buffetts of the world. The rest
> of us can give our talent, time, knowledge,
> contacts—whatever resources we have—to
> other worthy people in our lives at work and
> at home. We can act, instead of just watching
> others act or hearing about it in the news.*"
> —Cat Cassidy

I will philanthropize my life. I'll give of myself to worthy people and my GTY project(s) by:

1. Tithing my time
   - Committing to a specific percentage of my weekly time that I'll offer to my GTY project(s)
   - Being consistent in making my time available

2. Being clear on my intentions to make a difference in their lives by promoting their:
   - Welfare
   - Fortunes
   - Success
   - Capacity for achievement

3. Investing in the relationship
   - Declaring my desire to the recipient(s) and asking for their commitment to the relationship
   - Sharing my personal inventory and asking them to write and share theirs
   - Discovering and understanding their hopes and dreams
   - Demanding of myself to care about their hopes and dreams at least as much as my own

4. Giving it all away. I will open the floodgates and offer all of my:
   - Knowledge
   - Connections
   - Experience
   - Insights
   - Advice and counsel
   - Life lessons
   - Confidence
   - Words and gestures of encouragement
   - Tough and honest feedback

5. Holding them accountable to their commitments

REPLICATE YOURSELF

> *"Pay it forward, and demand that those you teach pay it forward, as well."*
> —Charles Roland

I will ensure that my GTY efforts expand far beyond my own relationships by:

1. Establishing the One Condition with my GTY recipient(s)
   - Make sure they understand that I expect nothing in return except that they take on GTY projects of their own.
   - Make sure they understand that *their* GTY project recipients will be required to take on GTY projects of *their* own.
   - Etc. to ∞

> **REPLICATE YOURSELF BY SHARING YOUR GTY EXPERIENCE**
>
> Consider using greaterthanyourself.com to post your successes and challenges as you pursue your GTY project.

2. Challenging everyone I know to practice GTY in their professional and personal lives

3. Sharing my GTY successes and failures with others, so they can learn from my experience

> > > > > > > **ACKNOWLEDGMENTS**

I'm blessed with a beloved cadre of friends and family—many of whom I've named specifically in my previous two books—who support and encourage me in more ways than I can even begin to catalogue. There are a few in particular, though, that had a direct hand in helping me with this particular endeavor. For them, I offer this shout-out with my deepest gratitude:

To my business manager, Kevin Small, for your astounding smarts and creativity, and to his cohort, Mat Miller, for your unwavering can-do approach to . . . well . . . everything.

To my agent, Jim Levine, for your authenticity.

To my marketing manager and de facto right hand, Andrea Temel, for your exuberant energy, lightning-speed responsiveness, and obsessive (in a good way) attention to all the details that matter.

To my editor, Roger Scholl, for your magic pen and patient understanding of the creative process.

To my longtime colleague Peter Alduino, who, once again, enriched this work with your priceless insights.

To Tommy "GTY Project" Spaulding, for all the reasons contained in this narrative, and then some.

To my brother, Bill, for your great feedback on earlier versions of this manuscript and for your belief in its value. Ditto to my sister, Mary.

To my all-grown-up kids, Saul, Jeremy, and Angelica, and to their still-growing-up "steppies," Kelsey, Heather, and Presley. I love watching you become more and more yourselves. May you all have lives much richer, deeper, fuller, and more joyous than mine. Which, believe me, is saying a lot.

To my wife, Veronica, for your devotion, support, and commitment to the things that are important in life.

And finally, to my friends in the blogosphere who were kind enough to respond—often times quite eloquently—to the early musings about GTY that I'd posted on my blog. Here, in the spirit of the blogging world, are their names. And since I can't insert hyperlinks into these paper pages, I encourage you to Google each one of them: David Pinter, Ann Stone, Scott Jensen, Patricia Mason, Mick Occhiuto, Neil Burgess, Jan Almarode, Ann Michael, Tim Johnson, Jim Koltveit, Tony Clark, Jodee Bock, Zane Safrit, Drew McLellan, Delaney Kirk, Morgan Ramsey, Tariq Khan, Dave J., Joshua Eubanks, Leslie Dorrans, Niels Teunis, Peter Jones, Stuart Cross, Greg Kittinger, John L. Herman, Jr., John Gregor, Christy Tonge, Candace Leuck, Claire Celsi, Bruce Dunning, Mike Sansone, Rebecca W., Asia Nelson, Michael Neely, Marc Grandle, Heidi Neilson, Billy Smith, Terry Starbucker, Liz Strauss, Kevin Eikenberry, Anna Farmery, Larry Hendrick, Dick Richards, Raj Setty, Roger Van Oech, Michael Wagner, Troy Worman, and the irrepressible Phil Gerbyshak.

I love you all.

ABOUT THE AUTHOR

STEVE FARBER, the president of Extreme Leadership, is a leadership consultant and speaker and the author of the national bestseller *The Radical Leap* as well as *The Radical Edge*. He lives in San Diego, California.

Be a part of something more and check out what is happening on **www.GreaterThanYourself.com.**

Visit the website and find your free resources today!

FREE GTY MUG
Remind yourself daily of the GTY objective by getting your free mug. Tell others in your workplace about GTY by using your mug as a conversation starter.

CHOOSING A GTY
Don't be intimidated by the idea of choosing a GTY project. Steve will answer your questions himself in this audio lesson. Learn how to best choose your GTY Project along with much more information.

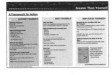

GTY POSTER
Inspire yourself after your done with the book to keep thinking GTY. Get this reminder of the book's key concepts and hang it at your desk or in your home. Remember to think Greater than Yourself.